4 Ways to Yummy
Children's Vegetable Cookbook

Garden to table veggie love

by Heide L. Horeth

Mandala, Ways to Enjoy Vegetables, Workbook Development and Design,
Facebook page, Illustrations
by Heide L. Horeth

Recipes by
Heide L. Horeth, Are West House and Marianne Borozny

Editing, website design, blog
Marianne Borozny

Publicity, Editing, Blog
Are West House

Layout and CGI by
Jerome H. Squire

ISBN 978-0-692-18706-7

Printed in PRC
First Printing, 2018
March Forth Publishing
Coupeville, WA. 98239
www.4waystoyummy.com

Disclaimer: The information, recipes, tips, advice and general content provided in **4 Ways to Yummy** is in no way intended, nor should be considered as, professional or medical advice. Please consult with your doctor and/or your child's dietician, nutritionist, GP or other medical professionals before changing your diet or lifestyle.

The editors and author of **4 Ways To Yummy** are in no way responsible for any direct, indirect, punitive, special, incidental or other consequential damages arising directly or indirectly from any use of this material.

4 Ways To Yummy reserves the right to change recipes, articles and information at any point without notification to its readers including the blog and website 4waystoyummy.com.

To the children -

our greatest leap of faith

whose imagination gives us laughter and hope

Why 4 Ways to Yummy?

4 Ways to Yummy Children's Vegetable Cookbook derives its name from the 4 unique and tasty recipes we feature with each vegetable. We've even dedicated a special page for each lead vegetable that will help children makes friends with veggies in 4 exploratory ways.

1) Explore the many ways the vegetable can be prepared and enjoyed by trying something new to you.
2) Our kitchen tool option suggestions may be used to vary texture in a recipe and make preparation more fun.
3) Spice partners suggestions we've listed all marry well with your choice vegetable. This category may be used as a spice substitution list for times when a change is desirable or necessary.
4) Fun facts that will help pique your curious nature and make you want to learn more about the fascinating tasty world of veggies.

Introduction

Having a child at 39 set the stage for a slower, simpler, grassroots kind of motherhood. My husband and I were still building our geodesic dome and we had 20 acres of land to yet tame. The birth of our son, Shane, took our lives in a most rich direction. How fun it was to be a part of the life cycle, and I vowed to not rush through those precious moments. I am not saying being a younger mother wouldn't have had its merits, but I can only be grateful for what I was experiencing at the time.

I eagerly brought my son into my adult world. Our days were spent picking branches in the yard, cooking supper, planting a small garden, reading stories, enjoying tea parties, and having gratitude. What else do parents want for their child, but health and slow, full days? I remember sometimes hiding books that we brought home from the library because they were just too stereotypical, outdated, and ridiculous to read again (and again). I thought even then I would love to write a story for my son that shared our values. Little did I know then that this idea would stick deep in my brain. After working ten years for a nurse and nutritionist in a very large progressive preschool, I saw the need for a healthful cookbook that was geared for children. One of my jobs at the school was drawing recipe charts and my colleagues would say, "We should write a cookbook." All this stayed inside me somewhere.

Fast forward to retirement, and a son who went off to college, and here we are! Old enough to have learned a few things, to be both opinionated and more accepting (okay, this is the hard one), but mostly having the time and desire to want to give back. This three-year journey has been a project of love. With the help of two friends, my journey began, changed, and now unfolds to you.

Knowing that the best foods for us are vegetables and that they are often the least appreciated, we decided to tackle and embrace vegetables in our **4 Ways to Yummy** cookbook. Each of our 12 featured vegetables is explored in 4 unique tasty ways,

Put veggies in the driver's seat of your meals by making them more appealing.
Serve them with simply cooked beans, grains, grilled fish or meat for a complete menu. We hope **4 Ways to Yummy** reconnects you to the healthful world of "rainbowlicious" vegetables.

Cooking with children is an important life skill to share and explore with them.
Your memories will be tasty too!

Table of Contents

Carrot

Cauliflower

Corn

the rainbow indicates an additional child friendly recipe page

Salad Dressings and Dipping Sauces

Thank a Farmer

Good food is undoubtedly one of life's greatest pleasures, and a commodity we simply could not live without! But do our children know where food comes from and how much effort it takes to bring it to our table? Vegetables do not come from the grocery store. Actually, they come from folks dedicated to nurturing seeds that have been planted in the ground. Today's average farmer feeds 155 people--a significant increase from 60 years ago, when that same farmer fed only 26 people. Their jobs are really a way of life, and their work is both humbling and inspiring.

Food appeals to us on so many levels. It's beautiful and primal, it smells fresh when it comes from the ground, and it's tasty and vital for our good health. We at **4 Ways to Yummy** wish to pause and thank our farmers for the important work they do--for bringing good food to our table.

In the Kitchen with Little Ones

When I was young everything seemed simpler and undoubtedly it was. Our parents and neighbors collaborated to teach us manners and keep us safe. While our work was to play hard with anyone who was available and let our imaginations guide us.

But it is a different world and each generation makes adjustments until the new way becomes the norm. I tried hard to fight some of the things I did not agree with but it wasn't always easy when you feel like you are all alone in the battle. However eating well is still possible and not difficult. And oddly (and happily) much of the older wisdom (like bone broths and fermented foods) are returning. Finding pleasure in healthy eating starts best when young, so let's see how we can implement cooking and healthy food with our little ones.

From the time I was very young, my mother would have me work alongside her in the kitchen. Before we began, she made sure I washed my hands and then gave me a small cutting board with a project. When I was able to safely handle a knife I would do some simple slicing but even as a very young child I could tear lettuce for a salad. Perhaps I might even get a piece of dough that I could knead and shape into my own creation. We would take turns mixing, filling or drying a dish. If my mother worked on the stove she would often pick me up to show me what was cooking and I marveled at her bubbling stews. We would taste soup together and I learned you could make adjustments to taste. Yes, cooking resulted in delicious creations and I wanted to do it!

So please let your little ones in on the process. At a young age, they can help set the table and carry dishes to the sink. Soon they can stir, spread, cut and create. In the kitchen, children will receive a feeling of accomplishment and realize they are a contributing and needed member of the family. Working together in the kitchen inspires conversation and ideas as well as laughter and memories. Start young, start slow and enjoy this journey. And I hope that when your child is 20, as my son is, he/she will be able to cook you a meal. And a delicious one at that!

Heide

Mandala is a Sanskrit word that means circle. "It is about the connection of all evolving elements both human and nature which revolve around the unifying center of the mandala". It represents wholeness.

This **Mandala** shows the 12 vegetable

Mandalas

What is a Mandala?

Mandala is a Sanskrit word that means circle. The vegetable **Mandala** reflects how all vegetables are a vital part in the quest for good nutrition. Color plays a vital role in nutrition and is nature's way to invite us to include a variety of foods into our diet for vibrant health.

This **Mandala** shows the 12 vegetables we will explore in our recipes. Can you name them all?

An Introduction to Vegetable Mandalas

Vegetable Mandala activities will help your entire family, from the youngest to the oldest, engage and explore the vegetable kingdom.

Children are often both curious and cautious about the unknown. This easy activity utilizes your child's curiosity while discovering all the delicious flavors, shapes, colors and intricacies of vegetables. Familiarizing and connecting children with how vegetables are grown, and how they look, feel and taste is key to getting them on the plate with interest.

Our mandalas are a science, technology, engineering and math (STEM) based activity. Use the mandala activity (there are no wrong answers) while in the vegetable aisle at the store, in your kitchen or in a vegetable garden. Approach vegetables from a fun, fresh and new perspective together as a family.

To help bring out the natural scientist in all of us, try using a magnifying glass when studying a vegetable. Notice the details you may have missed. Can you find a root or still see a trace of dirt? Be spontaneous and have fun spending quality time together! We think everyone will discover something new!

Vegetable Mandala I (A circle activity game of veggies)

As shown on the mandala, this activity is divided into four steps which spell **E A T S.**

Note: To play this activity, first select a vegetable to explore. Since carrots and beets are colorful, have edible tops and are available all year, they work well with this activity. Work your way clockwise around the Vegetable Mandala.

1. **E**xamine your vegetable like a detective. Look closely at the vegetable, list and discuss what you see or may already know. Use a magnifying glass, can you find a trace of soil? Does the veggie feel hard or soft? Smooth or rough?
2. **A**sk and encourage questions. What would you like to know? Does it grow above or below ground? What do plants need to grow? Do they all look exactly alike? Take a guess as to what's inside your vegetable. Do the parts all taste the same?
3. **T**ry your vegetable. Decide how you will eat a vegetable that may be new to you. Will you have a mouse's nibble or a brave bite? Will you try it raw or cooked? How does it feel on your tongue? Can you eat the flower and/or seeds?
4. **S**ummarize what you have learned. Take a minute to review and reflect on what you have discovered. Draw a picture of your vegetable; what shape is it? If you cooked a recipe, add your notes to **What I Think** at the end of your recipe. Rate your recipe, too. Did it get a smiley face? No? Could it if you changed something?

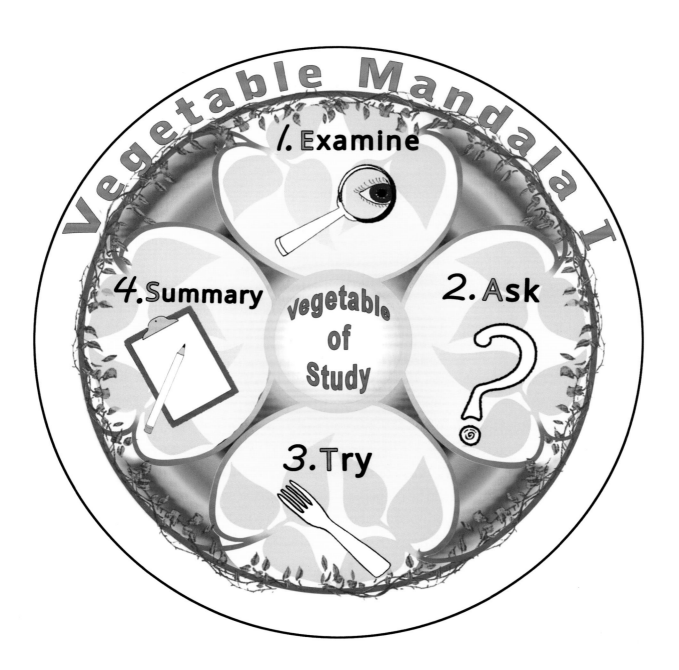

Vegetable Mandala II (A circle activity game of veggies)

Our **Vegetable Mandala II** is a more in-depth activity geared towards older children who would like to explore and expand their knowledge of vegetables. Follow the same 4 steps as in Vegetable Mandala I and explore on your own or try some of our suggestions.

1. **E**xamine - Use some math on your vegetable and see what it weighs and how large it measures. Does it have a root hair and could you measure its length? Dissect your vegetable and examine it inside thoroughly-is it the same color? Does it have seeds? Take good notes of your observations.

2. **A**sk - How many of this vegetable would it take to weigh as much as you (how about a grown up?)? Does this vegetable show tell tale signs of how it grew? Is it bruised from the journey it took? Can you visit a place where it is still growing in the ground? Do fresh, canned and frozen all taste the same? What animals eat this food? Why is it good for them and you? Does this vegetable look similar to another vegetable? Is it in the same family?

3. **T**ry - Approach the trying of your vegetable scientifically. What parts are edible? Does the vegetable taste the same from top to bottom and inside and out? I used to think the inner lighter core of a carrot tasted the sweetest. Do you? Do different colored vegetables taste the same (red, orange or yellow carrots)? The **Ways to Enjoy** vegetable page may be used as a reference to see the many ways a vegetable can be prepared (kitchen tools and seasonings). Which will you try?

4. **S**ummarize -Write down your observations and draw conclusions. Make a hypothesis? Maybe start a vegetable journal with sketches, detailed notes and recipes. Do interviews with family and friends to see what they think about the vegetable. If they didn't like it could you change their mind? Invent a recipe of your own: salad dressings and smoothies are a great way to start. What did you learn that you didn't know before? Are you becoming an expert on vegetables?

Vegetable Mandala II

Examine   Ask   Try   Summary

1 — Touch, Investigate Details, Smell, Texture, Weigh and Measure, ?

2 — What's inside?, Where does it grow?, What animals eat it?, What I'm curious about, Looks like?, ?

3 — Experiment, Food Courage, Use Tools, Make a Plan, Raw or Cooked?, ?

4 — Further Study, Create (invent) a recipe, Interview Family, What I Learned, Accept or Reject, ?

Shopping with Little Ones
How to make a Grocery List

3 carrots ☐

1 cucumber ☐

Romaine lettuce ☐

When going grocery shopping engage your child by having them make a grocery list of their own. Using a small clipboard is perfect for this task. You and your child can draw symbols and shapes to represent your items. Triangles for carrots and circles for tomatoes work very well. If your child can add a bit of color, the list quickly becomes a work of art. At the store let them be responsible for finding and picking out several items. Older children can do this on their own. Shopping with a list is a great way to show children how you plan and execute your menu, introduces a budget and discourages impulsive buying. When they ask for something you do not wish to buy you can simply tell them it is not on our shopping list . Show your child how to pick out the best produce. Vegetables have unique shapes and many colors. Maybe try a new one.

How to Wash Vegetables

A recent study has shown that baking soda makes an economical and effective way to remove pesticide residues both on the surface and below the skin. Soaking is the key as it took 12-15 minutes of soaking to completely remove the pesticides from apples in the study.

Taken from the Journal of Agricultural and Food Chemistry.
http://pubs.acs.org/doi/abs/10.1021/acs.jafc.7b03118?source=cen

The FDA still recommends washing produce under running water.

In our modern world we need to address the safety of our food. Even organic food can have pesticides, so washing our produce is the best defense to cleaner eating. Though the effect of ingesting chemicals through our food is conflicting and perhaps uncertain, we feel it makes sense to do what we can where food safety is concerned. Though soaking vegetables for 15 minutes may seem very long initially, it is likely that with practice this habit will become second nature. The soaking time can be used to read your recipe and assemble your ingredients. The overall work time to wash vegetables still totals just a couple of minutes.

1. Wash hands while singing *"Happy Birthday"* once or twice--20 seconds
2. Add 2-3 tsp baking soda to a large bowl of water
3. Add vegetables and swish
4. Soak vegetables about 12-15 minutes
5. Scrub vegetables
6. Rinse vegetables

Recipes

Beets

Storage: Keep the tails on beets when storing in the refrigerator, but do lop off any greens and store separately. The greens will draw the moisture out of the beets, making them age more quickly. Beetroots will last a good week or more in the crisper drawer. Tops should be used within a day or two.

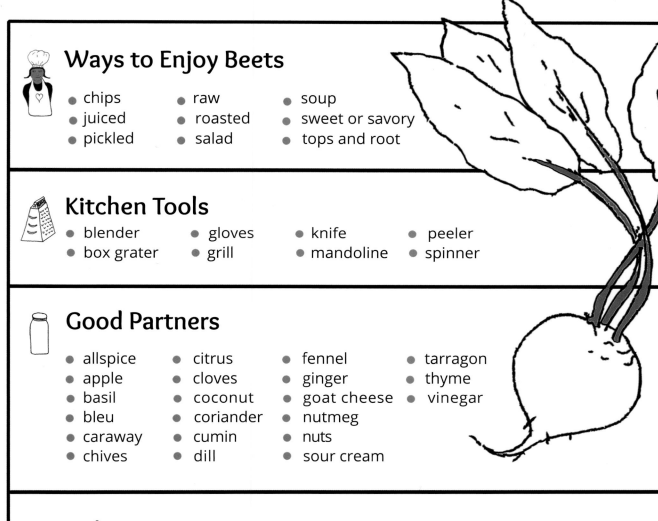

Ways to Enjoy Beets

- chips
- juiced
- pickled
- raw
- roasted
- salad
- soup
- sweet or savory
- tops and root

Kitchen Tools

- blender
- box grater
- gloves
- grill
- knife
- mandoline
- peeler
- spinner

Good Partners

- allspice
- apple
- basil
- bleu
- caraway
- chives
- citrus
- cloves
- coconut
- coriander
- cumin
- dill
- fennel
- ginger
- goat cheese
- nutmeg
- nuts
- sour cream
- tarragon
- thyme
- vinegar

Did You Know ?

Beets can dye fabric, eggs and even hair. Beet skins are bitter so if using raw, peel beforehand. If roasting beets, peel them afterwards as skins will slip away more easily. Red beets will stain your hands and everything else so wear gloves and cover surfaces. Golden beet varieties do not stain and tend to taste sweeter and less earthy.

What is beeturia? Can you guess?

Pachadi

What You Need:

1½ cups peeled and grated fresh beets
1 Tbsp oil
¼ cup sweetened coconut
½ mild green chili pepper or ¼ tsp dried red chili pepper
2 spring onions (white part only)
¼ tsp cumin
¼ tsp yellow or brown mustard seeds
Salt to taste
1½ cups yogurt (optional)

What You Do:

1. **Coconut Paste:** Grind the coconut in a food processor with choice of chili, onion, mustard seeds and cumin until the mixture is smooth. Add a little water if needed.
2. **Pachadi:** Add oil to a pan and saute the grated beetroot with a pinch of salt, and cook the beets until soft.
3. Add the coconut paste to the beets and mix well. After the mixture is cool, add in the yogurt (or leave it out if desired), and combine. Add water, if needed, to create a smooth consistency.

Serves 4. Pachadi is a nice accompaniment to rice.

Pachadi is a South Indian dish and similar to the North Indian dish raita.

The word pachadi broadly translates to food which has been pounded. It can be made from many kinds of cooked vegetables or fruits using yogurt and coconut paste. It is served with rice.

What I think!

Monkey's Yummy Beet Smoothie

What You Need:

1 small cooked beet
1 cup berries (strawberry, raspberry, blueberry)
½ banana
1 cup green kale or chard leaf, torn into small pieces, stems removed
1 tsp vanilla, orange, or lemon extract
1 Tbsp nut butter
½ Tbsp chia seeds (optional)
½ cup water and some ice as needed

What You Do:

Place the ingredients in blender and process until smooth.

Serves : 2 thirsty Chimpanzees.

20

1.

2.

3. Measure.

4. Peel and Cut.

5. Tear.

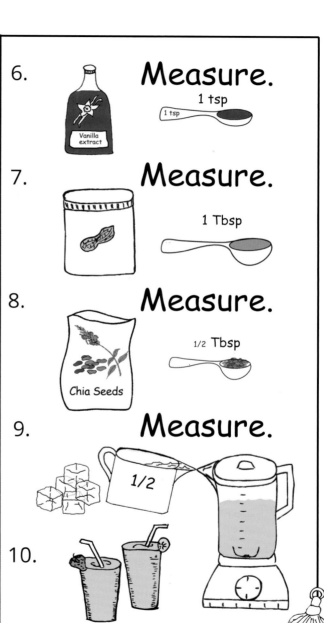

6. Measure.
1 tsp

7. Measure.
1 Tbsp

8. Measure.
1/2 Tbsp

9. Measure.
1/2

10.

Can't Beet 'Em Cupcakes

What You Need:

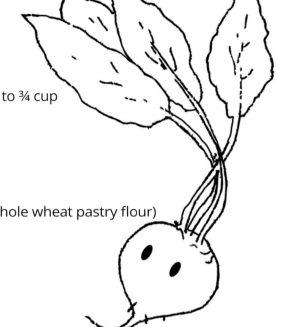

One 15 oz can of beets, drained, pureed and measured to ¾ cup

1 cup milk, plus 1 tsp vinegar*

¾ cup granulated sugar

¼ cup avocado oil or melted coconut oil

2 tsp pure vanilla extract**

1 cup plus 1 heaping Tbsp flour (unbleached white or whole wheat pastry flour)

Scant ½ cup unsweetened cocoa powder

1 tsp baking soda

½ tsp baking powder

Pinch salt

1 egg

2 generous Tbsp Nutella or peanut butter (optional, but gives cupcakes a better rise)

*unsweetened vanilla almond milk, coconut, whole milk, 2% milk or buttermilk **(If you are using buttermilk, eliminate the vinegar.)**

**We are purists when it comes to vanilla. The difference between artificial and pure is that the former has one flavor compound and the latter over 250 flavor compounds!

What You Do:

1. Preheat the oven to 375°F.
2. Grease a muffin tin or line it with paper liners.

22

3. Puree the drained beets and measure out ¾ of a cup.

4. In a large bowl, whisk together the wet ingredients (your choice of milk and the vinegar) and set it aside for a few minutes to curdle. **(If you use buttermilk, do not add vinegar.)**

5. Add the sugar, oil, egg, vanilla extract, optional Nutella or peanut butter and ¾ of a cup of pureed beets, and combine them until foamy.

6. Add the dry ingredients, flour, cocoa powder, baking soda, baking powder, and salt into a sifter and slowly sift the dry ingredients into a mixer or hand mix gently. Beat until no large lumps remain. It's important not to overbeat so cupcakes remain light.

7. Pour batter into pan 3/4 of the way full. Bake 22 to 25 minutes, or until a toothpick inserted into the center comes out clean. Do not unwrap until cooled or you will have sticky "paper" cupcakes.

8. Transfer pan to a cooling rack and let cupcakes cool completely.

9. Once completely cooled, dust with cocoa powder or powdered sugar and store in an airtight container. (They probably will never see a container, they will be gobbled up!)

Serves: 12-14 medium cupcakes

4 Variations: You might also try adding cinnamon, orange extract or cayenne pepper for a bit of heat. Using fresh cooked, cooled and grated beets makes this recipe more nutritious.

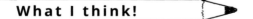

What I think!

23

BB Burgers (Beet and Bean)

What You Need:

¼ cup chopped onion
2 cloves garlic, minced
1 Tbsp cooking oil
½ cup finely chopped beets (canned or cooked and cooled)
¾ - 1 cup soft cooked rice (brown or white) and/or quinoa
¼ cup oats (roughly whirled in blender)
1 can kidney, white or pinto beans (drained and rinsed)
2 tsp smoked paprika
1 tsp prepared brown mustard
1 tsp cumin
1 Tbsp chia seeds
1 Tbsp barbeque sauce (optional)
Salt and pepper (dash)
1 egg, scrambled

What You Do:

1. Saute the onions and garlic in a little oil until they're nice and brown. Set aside.
2. Cook rice or quinoa until soft but not mushy. Set aside.
3. Using a food processor, whirl the drained and rinsed beans until they're almost smooth, but leave a little texture. You can also mash the beans by hand.
4. Add the rice, onions and chopped beets to the bean mixture.

5. Add the oats, paprika, mustard, cumin, barbeque sauce, salt, and pepper.
6. Taste and adjust the seasonings.
7. Add a scrambled egg to the mixture and combine well. The mixture should hold together nicely.
8. Form the mixture into thin patties, and cook them in a skillet with a little oil until they're heated through.

Serve on a bun and garnish with onion, tomato, aoli, etc., or eat as tapas.

Makes about 6 tasty burgers.

What I think!

Cabbage

Storage: Store this vegetable whole and unwashed in the crisper drawer. If cabbage is cut, wrap tightly. It will last 2-3 weeks. If the cabbage is shredded, use within a few days.

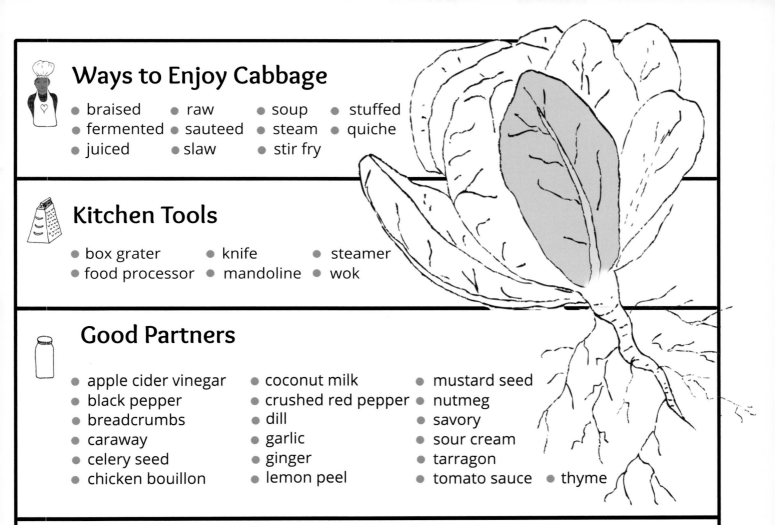

Ways to Enjoy Cabbage

- braised
- fermented
- juiced
- raw
- sauteed
- slaw
- soup
- steam
- stir fry
- stuffed
- quiche

Kitchen Tools

- box grater
- food processor
- knife
- mandoline
- steamer
- wok

Good Partners

- apple cider vinegar
- black pepper
- breadcrumbs
- caraway
- celery seed
- chicken bouillon
- coconut milk
- crushed red pepper
- dill
- garlic
- ginger
- lemon peel
- mustard seed
- nutmeg
- savory
- sour cream
- tarragon
- tomato sauce
- thyme

Did You Know ?

The largest cabbage on record weighed 138.25 lbs. grown in Alaska. One medium head equals about six cups of chopped cabbage. Cabbage is available in many varieties like Bok Choy, Cannonball, King, Savoy, Napa, or Red. One acre of cabbage yields more edible vegetables than any other crop because it only takes 3 months to grow.

It's cruciferous...what does that mean?

Cabbage Hash

What You Need:

½ small green cabbage
1 medium carrot, peeled and grated (optional)
1 to 2 Tbsp coconut oil
½ tsp coriander seed
2 tsp grated fresh ginger
1 tsp turmeric
½ tsp ground coriander
¼ tsp cumin
½ tsp paprika
Ground coconut (optional but so good)
Handful of chopped peanuts for garnish

What You Do:

1. Chop several cups of cabbage and set aside.
2. In a large pan heat oil on medium high, and add coriander seed and ginger and cook until fragrant, for about 1 to 2 minutes.
3. Add the rest of the spices. Stir together.
4. Add cabbage and mix well.
5. Add a few tablespoons water to help steam the cabbage. Cook for 2 to 6 minutes, depending on how much crunch you like your vegetable to have.
6. Sprinkle ground coconut and peanuts on top.

Serves 4 vegetarian elephants who love cabbage.

Variations:

Add in other veggies; try a handful of frozen or fresh peas or some grated carrot. Try chopped cashews, sesame seeds or peanuts on top. Try with a dash of our apple-ginger salad dressing on top. Goes well with fried potatoes.

What I think!

Spicy Korean Slaw

What You Need:

2 lbs. red and/or green cabbage, sliced thinly
½ medium sweet onion, sliced thinly
3 scallions, chopped
¼ cup cilantro, chopped
3 cloves garlic, minced
2 medium carrots, shredded
2 Tbsp soy sauce
1 Tbsp sesame oil
¼ cup rice vinegar (or to taste)
½ tsp crushed or powdered red pepper (We use Korean red pepper to taste--start small.)
2 Tbsp sugar
1 Tbsp sesame seeds (optional)
Salt and pepper to taste

What You Do:

1. Combine the cabbage, onion, scallions, carrots, cilantro, and garlic in a large bowl.
2. In a separate bowl, mix together all of the wet ingredients and sugar.
3. Sprinkle the red pepper on the dry ingredients.
4. Pour the wet ingredients onto the dry and mix them thoroughly.
5. Add salt and pepper to taste.
6. Sprinkle each serving with sesame seeds, if desired.

This slaw tastes even better the second day. You can make the dressing ahead of time to bring out the flavor.

Serves 8.

Red cabbage varieties can be used as a natural dye or used in kitchen science experiments. Here's a link: https://www.scientificamerican.com/article/bring-science-home-cabbage-chemistry/

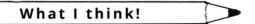
What I think!

Cabbage, A Love Story

Adapted from Molly Stevens' *All about Braising*

What You Need:

1-2 lb. head of cabbage, cut into 8 wedges
1 large carrot, cut into ¼-inch-thick rings
1 large onion, sliced thickly
¼ cup chicken or vegetable stock
¼ cup olive oil
⅛ tsp crushed red pepper (or to taste)
Coarse salt to taste
Freshly ground black pepper to taste

What You Do:

1. Preheat oven to 325°F.
2. Place the cabbage wedges in either an ovenproof pan or a casserole dish.
3. Spread the carrots and onions over the cabbage.
4. Mix the stock and olive oil together, and pour evenly over the vegetables.
5. Sprinkle a mixture of crushed red pepper, coarse salt and black pepper over the vegetable mixture.
6. Cover with a lid or foil, and braise in the oven for 1 hour. At the 1-hour mark, turn the cabbage over in the pan and re-cover. Braise 1 hour more.

7. Turn the oven up to 400°F. Remove the lid or foil and cook for 15 more minutes.

8. Sprinkle the cabbage with more coarse salt, if desired.

This dish tastes even better the second day.

Serves 6 to 8.

Did you know that our town of Coupeville just happens to be a huge supplier of cabbage seeds, and Washington state provides about 75% of the US production of cabbage seeds?

What I think!

COUPEVILLE

Whidbey Island

Cabbage Panade

A vegetable soup like dish thickened with bread
Adapted from Deborah Madison's *Vegetable Literacy*

What You Need:

3 Tbsp butter

1 medium onion, sliced thinly

2 lb. cabbage head (smooth green or savoy)

½ tsp juniper berries, crushed (If you can't find, try caraway, rosemary or black pepper.)

2 Tbsp sage leaves, coarsely chopped

3 ½ cups garlic stock (or use vegetable or chicken)

4 slices hearty, textured, light or dark rye bread

1 cup Swiss, Gruyere or milder Teleme cheese, grated

Salt and pepper to taste (Omit if using ready made stock bouillon.)

What You Do:

Garlic Stock

5 cups water

6 cloves garlic, lightly smashed

12 sage leaves

1 bay leaf

Simmer approximately 25 minutes. Strain.

Cabbage Panade

1. Preheat oven to 350ºF.
2. Melt butter in large skillet over medium heat. Add onion and saute until translucent.
3. Add juniper and sage and cook 10 minutes or until onion is nicely browned.
4. Add cabbage and half cup stock. Cook until cabbage is tender. Season with salt and pepper to taste.
5. Butter well a 2-quart ovenproof dish. Add half of cabbage to dish.
6. Top with bread slices torn to fit dish and add cheese. Add remaining cabbage and pour remaining stock over dish.
7. Bake until panade is nicely browned and bubbling for about 45 minutes. Serve in bowls to catch juices.

Variations: Chicken stock may be used in place of garlic stock. Cooked chicken or cooked sausage may also be added.

Serves 4-6.

Panade or panada is of Spanish origin, from the word pan which means bread. Variations of this dish are found in Britain, France and Italy.

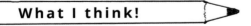
What I think!

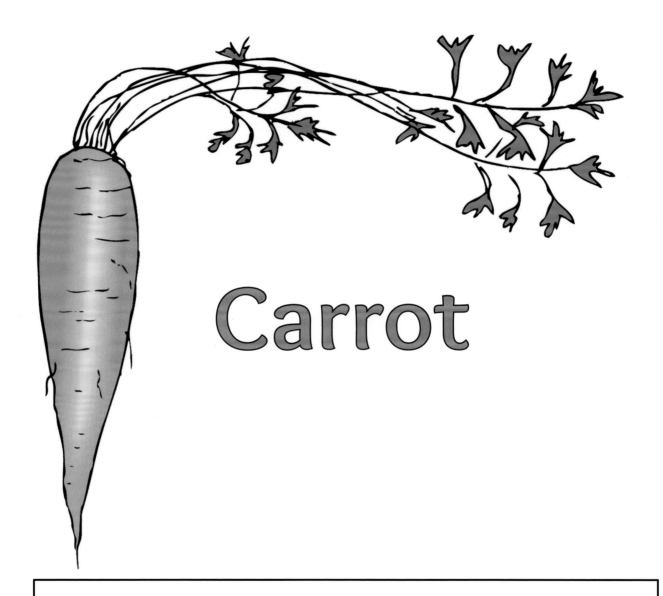

Carrot

Storage: To keep carrots freshest, cut off the green tops and store the taproot in water. Change water every few days.

Ways to Enjoy Carrots

- blanched
- chips
- dip
- juiced
- mashed
- puree
- raw
- roasted
- salad
- sauteed
- soup
- stews
- sweet/savory

Kitchen Tools

- box grater
- curler
- food processor
- hand masher
- knife
- mandoline
- peeler
- spiralizer
- steamer
- wok

Good Partners

- anise
- basil
- cardamom
- cinnamon
- citrus
- coriander
- cumin
- curry
- dill
- fennel
- garlic
- ginger
- honey
- mace
- nutmeg
- paprika
- parmesan
- parsley
- poppy seeds
- raisins
- rosemary
- sage
- shredded coconut
- sesame oil
- smoked paprika
- soy sauce
- sumac
- tarragon
- thyme
- vinegar

Did You Know?

Carrots come in white, yellow, orange, red and **purple.** Carrots were grown for medicine before food. The wild carrot is known as Queen Anne's Lace. The world's heaviest carrot weighed almost 20 lbs. Use carrots in spaghetti sauce to sweeten and help balance the acid from tomatoes.

Did you know there is a jelly bean flavor called carrot pie?

Bunny's Favorite Carrot Dip

What You Need:

3 or 4 large carrots, peeled and chopped into big pieces
1 whole clove garlic, peeled
¼ tsp cumin
¼ tsp paprika
¼ tsp ground ginger
1 small pinch cinnamon
1 small pinch cayenne
½ Tbsp honey
2 Tbsp lemon juice
1½ Tbsp olive oil
Salt to taste

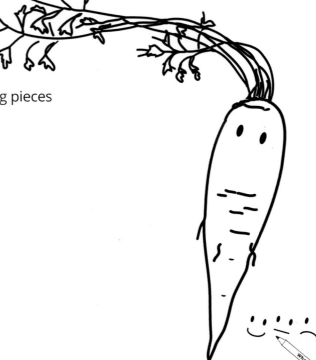

What You Do:

1. Cook the carrots with a clove of garlic on the stove top in water until the carrots are soft.
2. Drain the water and set the pot back on the stove for a few minutes to dry the vegetables. If needed, turn the heat back on.
3. Add the spices, honey and lemon juice to the carrots and garlic, and puree in a food processor.
4. While the food processor is running, add oil very slowly.
5. Taste and make any adjustments.
6. Let the dip cool.

Serve with crackers, vegetables or flatbread.

Serves a bunny garden party with four or more bunnies.

What I think!

Chunky Carrot Salad

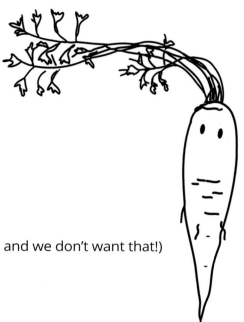

What You Need:

2 tsp Dijon mustard
1 Tbsp freshly squeezed lemon juice
1 ½ Tbsp vegetable oil
1 ½ Tbsp extra virgin olive oil
1 - 2 tsp honey, to taste
4 large carrots (Peel them or the carrots will be bitter, and we don't want that!)
Heaping ¼ tsp salt
¼ tsp freshly ground black pepper, or to taste
2 Tbsp chopped fresh parsley
2 finely sliced scallions, or 1 Tbsp finely chopped shallots (Green part only for scallions, please.)
A handful of golden raisins (Regular dark raisins will also do nicely.)
A small can of crushed pineapple, some of the juice drained

What You Do:

1. Grate the carrots in a food processor. (No processor? No problem! Get out your hand grater and let the kids grate and make a lovely orange pile of carrots! See **Grate Great Carrots** page 43)
2. In a salad bowl, combine the Dijon mustard, lemon juice (Oops! Catch those pits, or use a piece of cheesecloth over the lemon and squeeze. No pits!), honey, vegetable oil, olive oil, salt and pepper.
3. Toss in pineapple.

(continued on page 42)

Chunky Carrot Salad

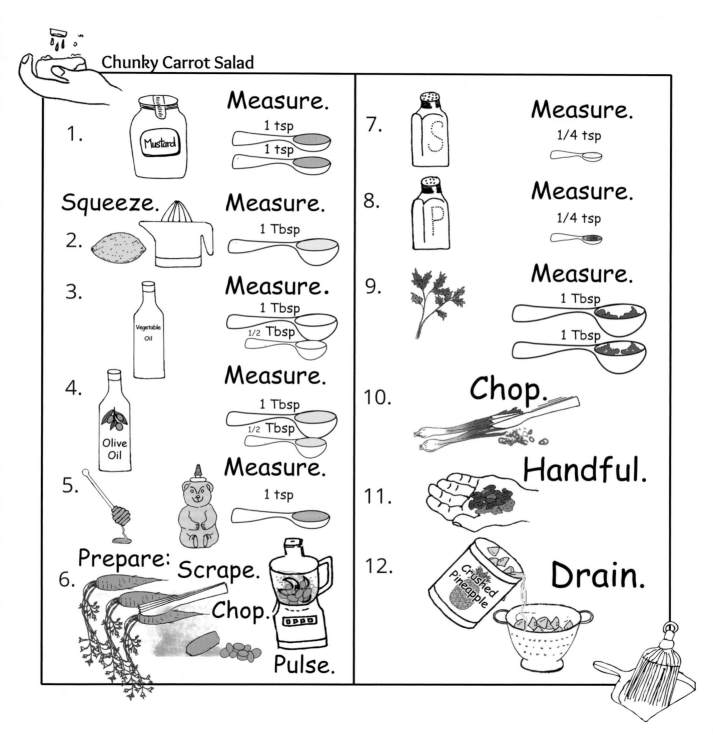

1. Mustard — Measure. 1 tsp / 1 tsp

2. Squeeze. — Measure. 1 Tbsp

3. Vegetable Oil — Measure. 1 Tbsp / 1/2 Tbsp

4. Olive Oil — Measure. 1 Tbsp / 1/2 Tbsp

5. Honey — Measure. 1 tsp

6. Prepare: Scrape. Chop. Pulse.

7. S — Measure. 1/4 tsp

8. P — Measure. 1/4 tsp

9. Measure. 1 Tbsp / 1 Tbsp

10. Chop.

11. Handful.

12. Crushed Pineapple — Drain.

4. Add the carrots, fresh parsley and scallions (or shallots). And now for the fun part: Have the kids (after washing their hands) toss the salad with their hands. The best chefs do and so do we!

Serves 4.

To plump: When raisins and other dried fruit get hard they can be soften and rehydrated again with a simple science trick. Place fruit in a heat proof cup and cover with boiling water, steeping for 5-10 minutes, then strain. The raisins will plump up again and be soft. Other liquids can also be used for plumping like sugar syrups that can be infused with flavorings such as vanilla or citrus or fruit juice.

What I think!

Grate Great Carrots

Originally invented for shredding cheese, the grater has proven itself to be a winner in the kitchen working magic with vegetables, fruits, eggs, garlic and even chocolate. In Jamaica the coconut grater has traditionally been used as a musical instrument. The grater is sometimes called the shredder. Box graters are a good choice for children to use because they are stable. However using caution will help children's fingers and knuckles from getting scraped or cut. We recommend for first timers that you choose a long vegetable to keep hands back from cutting area. Always have your child hold the vegetable firmly and go slowly up and down across cutting surface. Leave a healthy amount of vegetable uncut in order to keep some distance from the blades. Clean grater immediately with a brush or water before food dries into crevices (If dried on grater, try rubbing with a hard stale crusty bread to clean).

Most graters have 4 sides but some have more. How many does your have? What do they look like? Does it shred the pieces uniformly? Examine your results and taste them too.

How to grate:

1. Keep fingers clear of grater !!
2. Hold vegetable firmly.
3. Go firmly and slowly.
4. Cut larger vegetables into a managable size.

What do the different sides do?

What I think!

Hutspot

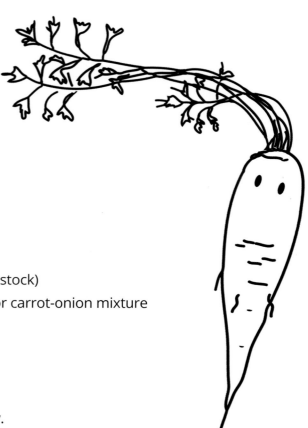

What You Need:

1 lb potatoes
1 lb carrots
½ lb onion
½ Tbsp butter
½ tsp sweet yellow curry powder
1 chicken or vegetable bouillon cube (or ½ cup stock)
Water (enough to cover potatoes) and ½ cup for carrot-onion mixture
Salt and pepper

What You Do:

1. Wash, peel and cut the potatoes uniformly.
2. Dice the onion and carrots.
3. Place the potatoes in a pot of salted water and cook until tender.
4. Heat the butter over medium heat and saute the onions until they're translucent.
5. Add the carrots, broken-up bouillon cube and ½ cup of water. Cook until the bouillon is dissolved and the carrots are tender.
6. Add the carrot-onion-bouillon mixture to the drained potatoes and curry powder.
7. Mash the mixture.
8. Add salt and pepper to taste.
9. Serve hot with a dollop of butter, or garnish as desired.

Serves 4.

Variation:

If you use cabbage instead of carrots, the dish is called Colcannon.

Hutspot is of Dutch origin that roughly translates to meaning "shaken pot." This is a typical winter dish possibly because using winter carrots makes this dish the tastiest. Other vegetable potato mashes can be tried like, cabbage, sweet potato, kale and parsnip.

What I think!

Rice is Nice Carrot Risotto

What You Need:

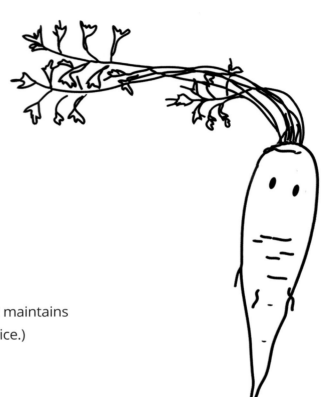

3 ½ cups chicken broth (approximately)
2 cups water
1 Tbsp olive oil
1 Tbsp butter
½ large onion, minced
6 medium carrots, grated
1¼ cups medium- or short-grained rice
   (We love Haiga rice--tastes like white but maintains
   many nutrients lost in traditional white rice.)
½ cup dry white wine (or use more broth)
¼ cup Parmesan cheese
Salt and pepper to taste

What You Do:

1. Heat the chicken broth and water to a simmer on stove. Keep the liquid warm.
2. In 1 Tbsp of oil in a large skillet and saute the onion and carrot until they're soft.
3. Add the rice and continue to saute for a few minutes.
4. Add the wine or more broth and cook for another minute until the liquid is absorbed.
5. Begin adding the broth mixture, 1 to 2 cups at a time, and simmer until the liquid is absorbed.
6. Continue to add broth until the rice is creamy, 20 to 30 minutes.

7. Remove from stove and stir in the butter and Parmesan cheese.

8. Season with salt and pepper as desired.

Serves 6.

Risotto is the most common rice dish originating from Italy around the 15th century. It is made by cooking rice with broth until it is a creamy consistency. The word comes from the Italian word riso meaning rice. Variations can include the addition of cheese, butter, onion, vegetables or meat.

What I think!

Cauliflower

Storage: To keep it fresh longer, store heads in the refrigerator unwashed and facing downward...it's shy.

Ways to Enjoy Cauliflower

- casseroles
- dip
- mashed
- pickled
- pizza crust
- raw
- riced
- roasted
- salad
- soup
- steamed
- stir fried

Kitchen Tools

- box grater
- food chopper
- food processor
- grill
- knife
- masher
- stalk chopper
- ricer

Good Partners

- basil
- five spice
- cilantro
- cinnamon
- citrus
- coriander
- cumin
- dill
- fennel
- garlic
- ginger
- harissa
- lime
- mint
- mustard
- nutmeg
- olives
- oregano
- paprika
- parsley
- sage
- sesame oil
- smoked paprika
- sumac
- tarragon
- thyme
- turmeric
- Zaatar

Did You Know ?

Cauliflower comes in orange, **purple**, green and white . All varieties are healthful, and their tastes are very similar, but their colors give them unique nutritional characteristics. The color of the white variety is due to the leaves of the plant shading it from the sun. In the Guinness Book of Records, the largest cauliflower measured six feet across and 60 lbs. 9.3 ounces. It was grown in Newark, East Midlands, UK.

How many cauliflowers are you in pounds?

Cauliflower Pilaf

What You Need:

1 head cauliflower (about 4 cups coarsely grated - core removed if desired)
½ onion, minced
1 Tbsp butter
1 - 2 cloves garlic, minced
½ cup chicken stock
¼ - ½ cup golden raisins
¼ - ½ cup slivered or chopped almonds
¼ cup chopped parsley
Salt and pepper to taste

Variations: ¼ tsp cinnamon, ¼ tsp cardamom, ¼ tsp ground ginger, ¼ tsp turmeric, and/or 1 Tbsp lemon or orange zest. Regular raisins work, too.

What You Do:

1. In a large pan, saute the onions in butter over medium-high heat until soft. If using optional spices, add them in with the cauliflower and saute for about four minutes.
2. Add the garlic and cauliflower and cook for another minute.
3. Add the chicken stock and continue to cook until the cauliflower is tender, about 3-5 minutes.
4. Add the raisins, nuts and parsley, and mix and serve. If desired, add the lemon or orange zest at this stage.

Serves 6.

Variations: You can grate the cauliflower core and add it to the pilaf, or save it and serve raw like a radish. You can also use the leaves by sauteing them with a little butter and garlic. The whole cauliflower is edible and delicious. Cauliflower leaves are delicious. They can be roasted in a 400°F oven for approximately 25 minutes. Enjoy warm and crispy, or saute the leaves in butter with garlic.

The history of pilaf predates written history. It may have originated in India or from Persia. Pilaf refers to a rice dish cooked in seasoned broth with something added. It could be cooked vegetables, meat, fish, pasta, lentils, potatoes or dried fruit Spiced yogurt often accompanies this dish. In some cultures pilaf is served at weddings and other special occasions and was known to have been served to Alexander the Great.

What I think!

Big quantity.

Cauliflower Tomato Soup

What You Need:

3 Tbsp vegetable oil
1 tsp ground mustard seeds
½ tsp ground turmeric
1½ tsp ground cumin
½ tsp red pepper flakes, or to taste
2 tsp ground coriander
1 medium white or yellow onion, chopped
1 28 oz. can crushed tomatoes
1½ lbs fresh or frozen cauliflower, cut into florets
3½ cups water
½ to 1 tsp kosher salt, or to taste
¼ tsp freshly ground black pepper
Grated ginger to taste (optional)
½ cup plain yogurt
½ cup cilantro leaves, chopped

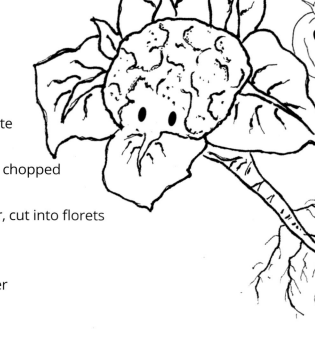

What You Do:

1. In a 4-quart stock pot, add vegetable oil, mustard, turmeric, cumin, red pepper flakes, and coriander. Over medium heat, gently warm the spices until you begin to smell their aroma.
2. Add onions and reduce the heat to medium-low, and cook until the onions are soft, about 5–6 minutes.

3. Add crushed tomatoes, cauliflower and water. Increase heat to high, and bring to a boil. Reduce heat to low, cover, and cook until the cauliflower is soft, about 25–30 minutes.
4. Remove from heat, cool slightly, and use an immersion blender, food processor, or regular blender to create a smooth, "creamy" soup with half of the cauliflower mixture. Add to other half of the cauliflower mixture. Season with kosher salt and black pepper. Garnish with cilantro and yogurt.

Serves 6.

What I think!

"Collie Flower" Pizza Crust

What You Need:

2½ cups cauliflower, coarsely grated (about ½ large head)
1-2 Tbsp flour (if needed)
1 large egg
1¼ cups mozzarella (Save ¼ cup for topping off pizza.)
2 Tbsp grated Parmesan
1 cup marinara sauce or any pizza sauce (You can use our marinara sauce recipe here.)
Kosher salt to taste
Red pepper flakes to taste
2 cloves garlic, chopped or minced. We are garlic people, so we love it chopped.
Chopped veggies and/or toppings of choice
1 tsp oregano
Fresh basil leaves
Sprinkle of flour (if needed)

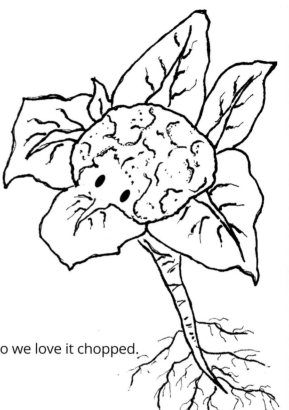

What You Do:

1. Preheat the oven to 425°F.
2. Line a rimmed baking sheet with parchment paper.
3. Grate the cauliflower using a box grater until you have two cups of cauliflower crumbles. Cook in a microwave or steam until soft. Remove and let the cauliflower crumbles cool.
4. Mix in the egg, 1 cup of mozzarella, parmesan cheese, and cauliflower (flour, if needed), and salt and pepper. Once combined, pat and flatten the mixture into a 10-inch round on

the prepared baking sheet. Spray lightly with nonstick spray or brush with oil and bake for 10 to 15 minutes or until golden.

5. Top the pizza crust with the sauce, oregano, veggies, (you can sneak some pepperoni in here) garlic and red pepper flakes. Add the ¼ cup of remaining mozzarella. Bake in the oven until it's melted and bubbly, about 5-7 minutes. Top with basil before serving.

Serves 6 children or 4 medium collies.

Baked Cauliflower

What You Need:

3 cups lightly cooked and drained cauliflower florets (al dente)
2 Tbsp cream cheese (room temperature)
3 rounded Tbsp cottage cheese
Dash of pepper, salt and nutmeg to taste

Topping:

1 Tbsp butter
¼ cup breadcrumbs

What You Do:

1. Preheat oven to 350°F.
2. Add cheeses and seasonings to cooked cauliflower. The warm vegetable will help blend the cheeses as you gently combine.
3. Spoon the mixture into a greased 8x8" ovenproof baking dish.
4. In a saute pan over medium heat, melt the butter, add the breadcrumbs and cook until they're toasted to a light golden brown. Be careful to not overcook as browning happens quickly.
5. Sprinkle the breadcrumb mixture on top of the casserole, and place in oven for approximately 20 minutes.

Variations: Substitute paprika for nutmeg. For a drier, smoother preparation, substitute ricotta for cottage cheese.

Serves 4.

For a simple **roasted cauliflower** cut a 2 lb. cauliflower into 8 wedges. Coat pieces with 2 Tbsp. olive oil. Add salt and pepper. Roast in 400° oven for about 12 minutes, then flip over and roast another 12 minutes. Goes well with pasta!

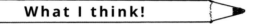 **What I think!**

Corn

Storage: To store fresh corn, refrigerate immediately, leaving husk intact. If there is no husk wrap it up to keep the corn from drying out. Eat as soon as possible or within a few days. Brown sticky tassels and bright green tight husks are a good indication of fresh corn.

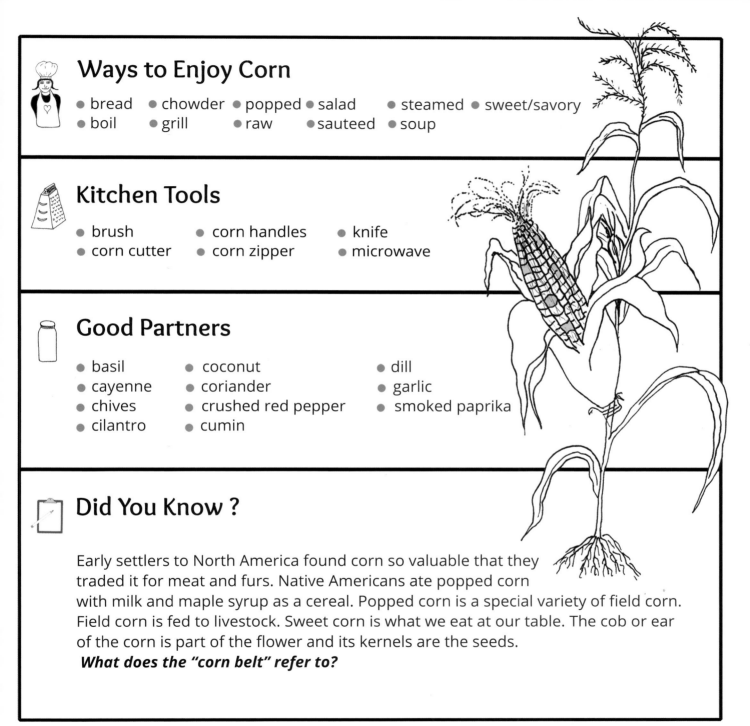

Ways to Enjoy Corn

- bread
- chowder
- popped
- salad
- steamed
- sweet/savory
- boil
- grill
- raw
- sauteed
- soup

Kitchen Tools

- brush
- corn handles
- knife
- corn cutter
- corn zipper
- microwave

Good Partners

- basil
- coconut
- dill
- cayenne
- coriander
- garlic
- chives
- crushed red pepper
- smoked paprika
- cilantro
- cumin

Did You Know ?

Early settlers to North America found corn so valuable that they traded it for meat and furs. Native Americans ate popped corn with milk and maple syrup as a cereal. Popped corn is a special variety of field corn. Field corn is fed to livestock. Sweet corn is what we eat at our table. The cob or ear of the corn is part of the flower and its kernels are the seeds.

What does the "corn belt" refer to?

Crazy Corn & Buttery Basil Saute

What You Need:

3½ cups fresh corn kernels (The middle of winter? No fresh corn?
No problem--just use canned frozen corn, drained and rinsed.)
1/3 cup chopped shallots
1 Tbsp butter (You can use olive oil, but we prefer butter,
which gives it a richer flavor, like eating corn on the cob.)
1/4 cup fresh basil leaves, chopped
1 medium red pepper (for color) chopped
2 cloves garlic, finely chopped
Salt to taste

What You Do:

1. Saute the corn kernels, shallots and red pepper in butter in large nonstick skillet over medium-high heat for 2 minutes.
2. Add the garlic and cook 1 minute longer.
3. Transfer to a serving bowl and stir in the basil. Season to taste.

Variation: Complements cooked quinoa or rice.

Serves 4.

What I think!

Scarecrow's Cornbread

What You Need:

1 cup yellow medium to fine grind cornmeal
½ cup flour
2 Tbsp sugar
2 tsp baking powder
¼ tsp turmeric (optional)
½ tsp salt
¾ cup canned creamed corn
¼ cup butter, melted (slightly cooled)
1 egg, beaten

What You Do:

1. Preheat oven to 400°F.
2. Grease an 8-inch square pan well.
3. In a large bowl add cornmeal, flour, sugar, baking powder, and salt. Mix well.
4. Melt ¼ cup of butter with or without turmeric. Cool.
5. Add the corn, melted butter, and egg. Combine gently until the batter is just blended.
6. Scrape the batter into the pan and bake until the edges pull away, approximately 20 min.
7. Cool on a rack.

Serves 8.

What I think!

Hot Tomato and Corn Pie

What You Need:

8 oz frozen corn (We prefer white.)
2-3 large ripe tomatoes, chopped
2-3 Tbsp olive oil
Pre-made pie crust
1 oz butter, melted, for brushing crust
⅓ cup cornmeal
½ fresh red bell pepper, chopped
I large egg (beaten)
¼ cup shredded cheese
¼ cup basil, chopped
1-2 Tbsp oregano, chopped (Fresh is best.)
Dash of salt and pepper
⅛ tsp chili pepper to taste
1/16 tsp (smattering) of crushed red pepper

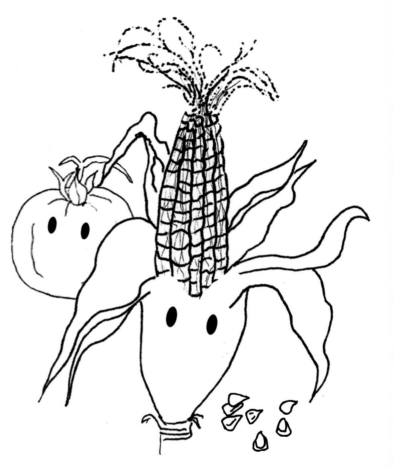

What You Do:

1. Preheat oven at 350°F.
2. Roll out the pie crust, brushing melted butter on the crust.
3. Sprinkle on the cornmeal until it sticks to the crust.
4. Place the pie crust in ovenproof dish, and set aside.
5. Use the bowl of a spoon to flute the edges of the pie.

6. Chop up the tomatoes, basil, red pepper and oregano.
7. Saute the veggies gently in olive oil. (Don't overcook them.)
8. Place the veggies, spices, beaten egg, and cheese in a bowl and gently mix.
9. Pour the mixture into the pie shell.
10. Bake for about 40 minutes.

Serves 8.

The cob or ear of corn is part of the flower, and its kernels are the seeds. On average, an ear of corn has 800 kernels and 16 rows. There are always an even number of rows. Care to count for yourself?

What I think!

Cracklin' Corn Fritters

What You Need:

2 cups corn, fresh or frozen

½ cup cornmeal, fine or medium

1 cup flour

1 chopped fresh green chili pepper

(or a plain old green pepper will do as well)

2 tsp finely chopped or grated ginger

½ tsp red pepper flakes

¼ tsp cumin

2 Tbsp chopped cilantro

2 tsp lemon juice

½ tsp Kosher salt

2 tsp olive oil

1 egg

¼ cup of water

½ tsp baking powder

¼ cup melted butter

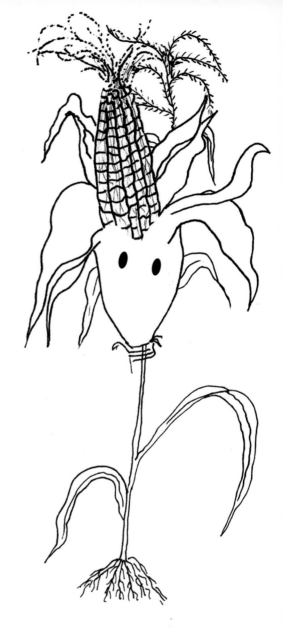

What You Do:

1. If using frozen corn, thaw in hot water and drain.
2. Add cornmeal, flour, chili, cilantro, ginger, lemon juice, cumin seeds, and salt to corn, and mix well by hand. Mixture should be consistency of thick batter. Add a little water if needed.

3. Heat a heavy skillet on medium heat and generously grease skillet with olive oil.
4. Drop about 2 spoonfuls of batter to make 4 to 5 patties into skillet. Make each patty about 1/4 inch thick and 2 to 3 inches wide. Flip gently when center is bubbly and edges are crispy about 2 to 3 minutes.
5. Serve them hot or at room temperature.

Variations: These are delicious with just a bit of melted butter, but pure maple syrup works well too. We also enjoy a side of applesauce with our fritters. These are great as a finger food after school snack.

Serves 2- 3 adults (about 2 fritters per person).

The word fritter comes from Latin word frictura which means to fry. Fritters are essentially fried batter concoctions. Usually made from vegetables, fruit, seafood or meat that has been chopped, minced or left whole then dipped in batter and fried in oil. Flower fritter are also popular and have been made from dandelions, daylilies, roses, violets, acacia, elderberry and courgette (zucchini) blossoms.

What I think!

Green Beans

Storage: Store green beans unwashed in a plastic bag in the refrigerator for up to a week.

Ways to Enjoy Green Beans

- baked fries
- blanched
- casserole
- grilled
- pickled
- roasted
- salad
- sauteed
- soup
- steamed
- stir fried

Kitchen Tools

- Bean Frencher
- hands
- knife
- wok

Good Partners

- basil
- chives
- cinnamon
- crushed red pepper
- dill
- garlic
- marjoram
- mustard
- nutmeg
- oregano
- parsley
- pepper
- rosemary
- savory
- sesame seeds or oil
- smoked paprika
- thyme
- vinegar

Did You Know ?

There are more than 130 varieties of green beans; they can look and taste differently. Bean pods are not always **green** ; they can be **purple**, yellow, **red** or **mottled**. Green beans are an annual plant with a life cycle that completes in one year. Beans are the only cultivated plant that enriches the soil. The English language has a number of fun expressions that use the word bean, such as "spill the beans," "full of beans" and "I've been beaned."

Do you know what these expressions mean?

Sandy Beach Noodles

What You Need:

2 cups cooked green beans
2 Tbsp butter
1/4 cup regular bread crumbs
3 cups any variety cooked egg noodles
Salt, pepper to taste

What You Do:

1. Heat the butter in a large skillet over medium heat. When the butter is hot, add in the breadcrumbs and toast until golden brown. Do not leave the mixture unattended because the crumbs can turn from a nice brown to burnt pretty quickly.
2. Cook the noodles according to directions, drain and toss them into the bread crumb mixture. Make sure there is a bit of moisture on the noodles as this will help the breadcrumbs stick.
3. Clean and cut the beans into a manageable size. Boil or steam the beans on the stove until they're crisp and tender, 4 or 5 minutes.
4. When they're ready, toss the beans with the noodles to coat them evenly. Cook until warmed through.

Serve hot.

Serves 4.

Variations:

Can be made with a mix of vegetables like cauliflower, carrots, peas and cooked greens. It's a great way to use up leftover vegetables, too.

As a child, we would eat just the bread crumb-covered noodles with a dusting of powdered sugar on top and a side of applesauce. My son's friends all loved this dish. It's fast and economical to prepare.

Homemade Breadcrumbs

Save unused bread and make your own breadcrumbs for free. They are much tastier than store bought. Slice bread into thin slices or use sliced bread and dry in 250-300ºF oven for 10-15 minutes or until dry and crispy. Run pieces through a food processor.

You can also make breadcrumbs by hand by putting bread pieces in a bag and crushing them with a rolling pin. These will store for up to a year in a storage container at room temperature.

What I think!

Greek Green Beans

What You Need:

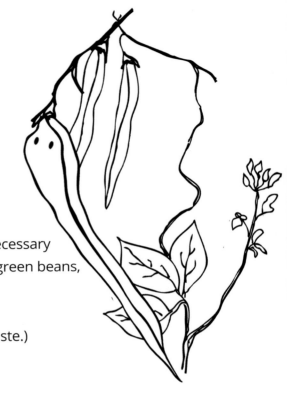

1-2 Tbsp oil

⅓ cup onion, minced

1 clove garlic, minced

1 Tbsp tomato paste

¼ cup chicken or vegetable stock or water; add more if necessary

16 oz fresh or frozen green beans, or 14.5-ounce canned green beans, drained/rinsed

10-oz can diced or crushed tomatoes

1 tsp cumin or dill (Dill is a bit sweeter--more of a citrus taste.)

15 oz canned garbanzo beans, drained/rinsed

Handful of chopped almonds (optional)

Dash of cayenne or tsp paprika (optional)

Salt to taste

What You Do:

1. Heat the oil over medium heat and saute the onion until softened and lightly browned, about 6-7 minutes.
2. Add the garlic and saute another minute or two.
3. Add the tomato paste and stock, stir until combined.
4. Add green beans, drained garbanzos, tomatoes , almonds and spices.

5. Cover the pan and simmer over low heat for 30 to 45 minutes, until the beans are at the desired tenderness. Fresh or frozen green beans only need to be heated through until flavors have melded, approximately 10 minutes.

Serves 6.

Variations: Substitute crushed tomatoes with chili peppers for a spicier version of this dish. You may also puree the tomatoes for a smoother texture.

Serve with crumbled feta cheese or plain yogurt on top, if desired.

Puree: To make a food into a creamy smooth consistency by a process like blending. Foods like hummus, baby food, applesauce and tomato sauce are examples of pureed foods. Can you name another?

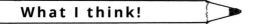

What I think!

Sweet and Sassy Green Beans

What You Need:

Splash of high temp oil. I like algae, peanut or avocado.
1 lb. green beans washed and cut to desired length.
½ can to 1 can water chestnuts, drained and chopped.

Sauce:

1 Tbsp rice vinegar
1 Tbsp soy sauce
1 Tbsp Hoisin sauce

Mix all three ingredients together.

What You Do:

1. Stir fry green beans in a splash of oil until almost cooked, 3-5 minutes.
2. Add sauce and the water chestnuts and cook briefly until heated through.

Can be eaten hot or cold.

Serves 4.

72

Sweet and Sassy Green Beans

1. Wash.

1 lb.

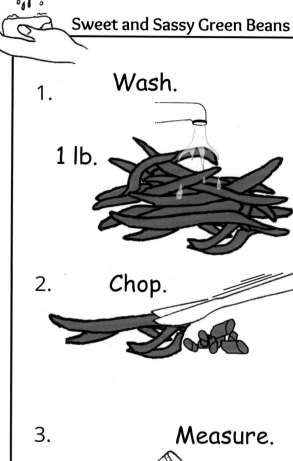

2. Chop.

3. Measure.

Rice Vinegar   1 Tbsp

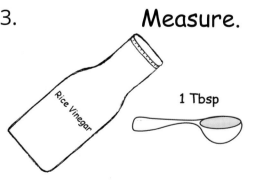

4. Measure.

Soy Sauce   1 Tbsp

5. Measure.

Hoisen   1 Tbsp

6. Mix.

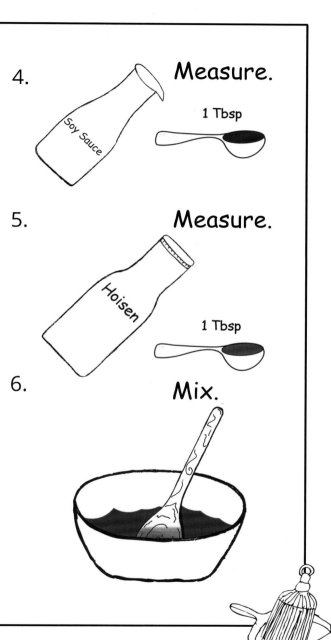

Roasted Soy Sesame Green Beans

What You Need:

1 lb. fresh green beans, ends trimmed
3 cloves garlic, minced or pressed
2 Tbsp soy sauce
2 tsp vegetable oil (We used peanut oil.)
1 tsp sesame oil
¼ tsp ground black pepper

What You Do:

1. Place all of the ingredients in a shallow dish and mix well. Marinate for 1 hour.
2. Preheat the oven to 425°F. Place a sheet pan in the oven for 10 minutes.
3. Spread the green bean mixture across the sheet pan
4. Roast for 12-15 minutes, turning the pan around at the halfway point.
5. Serve this dish right away for the best texture.

Serves 4

What I think!

Roasted Soy Sesame Green Beans

1. **Wash and trim tips.**

   1 lb.

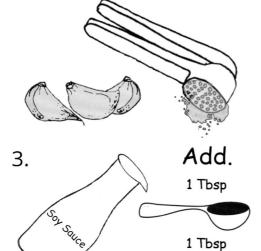

2. **Mince or Press.**

3. **Add.**

   1 Tbsp

   1 Tbsp

   Soy Sauce

4. **Add.**

   1 tsp

   1 tsp

   Peanut Oil

5. **Add.**

   1 tsp

   Sesame Oil

6. **Add.**

   ¼ tsp

7. **Mix and Marinate.**

   1 hr

Kale

Storage: Remember to keep kale cold and store in the refrigerator. At room temperature kale can get bitter. I wrap my unwashed kale loosely in a damp paper towel and then put it in a plastic bag. Use within a few days.

Ways to Enjoy Kale

- baked
- dip
- juiced
- pesto
- raw
- salad
- sauteed
- smoothie
- stew
- stir fried
- stuffed
- soup
- quiche

Kitchen Tools

- blender
- hands (strip, tear, massage)
- knife
- salad spinner
- wok

Good Partners

- basil
- bay leaf
- chicken stock
- coconut milk
- coriander
- crushed red pepper
- cumin
- curry
- feta
- garlic
- ginger
- lemon
- marjoram
- mustard seeds
- nuts
- nutmeg
- oregano
- rosemary
- vinegar
- sesame seeds or oil
- smoked paprika
- sour cream
- soy sauce
- turmeric

Did You Know ?

This vegetable can be **purple**, white, **green**, or **bluish.** Kale is considered a superfood because it has one of the highest antioxidant levels of any vegetable. Some vegetables like kale have a sweet defense to cold weather. Kale reacts to the cold by producing sugars. Some root vegetables (like carrots) also taste sweeter after a frost because these plants react by converting some of their starches to sugar.

Did you know kale is also used in skin products and nail polish?

Kale-Pineapple-Banana Lassi

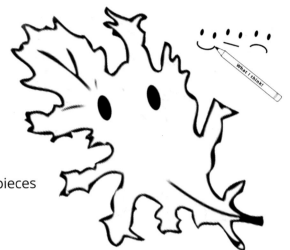

What You Need:

½ cup water or 5 ice cubes
½ cup coconut milk or ½ plain yogurt
1 ½ cups torn kale, chard or spinach, torn into small pieces
1 cup pineapple, chopped
1 ripe banana

What You Do:

Combine all ingredients in a blender and pulse and blend until smooth. Add more water if too thick.

Serves 2 thirsty forest sprites

Lassi is an ancient "smoothie" originating in India from around 1000 BC. It is made by blending water with yogurt then adding in fruits, spices, salt or sweeteners. It can be sweet or savory. Chaati Lassi another version of a "smoothie" from India is made from buttermilk. Drinking lassis are said to have a calming effect on the stomach.

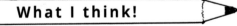

What I think!

Kale-Pineapple-Banana Lassi

1.

2. **Measure.**

3. **Measure.**

4. **Tear.**

5. **Chop.**
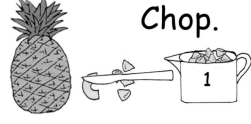

6. **Peel.**

7. **Blend.**

8.

Kickin' Kale and Quinoa

What You Need:

½ cup quinoa

1 cup chicken broth (We prefer vegetable broth, and we save leftover juice from the cooked veggies and freeze it.)

1 Tbsp olive oil

1 onion, chopped

1 tsp turmeric

¼ tsp cumin

2 cloves garlic, finely chopped

5 to 6 cups kale, stripped from the stem (We chop ours small since kale can be a rough on the palate if the pieces are too big.)

½ tsp red pepper flakes or to taste

Pinch of sea salt or any salt you have on hand

2 Tbsp Parmesan cheese, grated

2 Tbsp panko breadcrumbs

What You Do:

1. Rinse and soak quinoa for about 10 minutes in warm water.
2. Bring 1 cup of chicken broth to a boil in a small saucepan.
3. Drain and add quinoa to boiling broth.
4. Cover and reduce heat to a simmer, cooking for about 15 minutes or until broth is absorbed.

5. Turn off heat and allow quinoa to sit for an additional 5 minutes, and then fluff with a fork. Set aside.
6. In a large skillet, drizzle olive oil over medium heat, and saute the onion and garlic until they are fragrant.
7. Add kale along with 2 Tbsp of water, and cover. Allow kale to steam for about 5 to 10 minutes, stirring occasionally until it is tender.
8. Remove lid and add 1 cup cooked quinoa, a pinch of salt, and all spices, mixing well.
9. Add Parmesan cheese and breadcrumbs, cooking until cheese is melted, and then serve immediately!

Variation: Add leftover chicken for those meat eaters! Also, try mustard greens instead of kale.

Serves 4-6.

What I think!

Ricotta Kale Balls

What You Need:

1½ cups cooked, finely chopped kale or spinach
½ cup onion, sauteed
2 tsp vegetable oil for onions
1 egg
½ cup breadcrumbs or panko
2 Tbsp grated Parmesan cheese
4 Tbsp ricotta cheese
Salt and pepper (generous dash)

What You Do:

1. Preheat oven at 350°F.
2. Cook the kale either by blanching and then squeezing out the excess water or by sauteing it with onions.
3. Mix all ingredients together in a large bowl.
4. Use hands to form 1-inch balls.
5. Place balls in a greased ovenproof dish.
6. Bake for about 15 minutes.
7. Flip balls and bake for approximately another 15 minutes. They should be lightly browned.

Serve kale balls hot with our Sassy Saucy Marinara or spread them on a sliced baguette. Sprinkle grated Parmesan on top.

Makes about 16 balls.

Serves 4.

Variation: Garlic powder, minced garlic, and/or crushed red pepper to taste.

What I think!

Hail Kale Salad

What You Need:

1 medium bunch kale, stems removed, chopped small
½ cup crumbled feta or soft goat cheese
½ cup chopped or small nuts: walnuts, pine nuts, pecans, almonds
½ cup dried fruit: cranberries or tart cherries
2 Tbsp lemon juice
2 Tbsp olive oil
Salt to taste

What You Do:

1. Wash and dry the kale thoroughly.
2. Massage kale   (See next page)
3. Mix in the remaining ingredients, folding in the cheese gently.
4. Salt to taste.

Serves 4-6.

Variation: Try bleu cheese! Use Satsuma oranges! Kale is a very forgiving vegetable.

What I think!

How to Massage Kale

The word massage generally means to rub, squeeze or knead parts of the body with one's hands. Medically this is done to help muscles, joints and people to feel better. In cooking terms massaging is done much the same way. It helps tougher greens become softer and more digestible. It also makes the color turn a vibrant green-like magic! You will also notice that the salad shrinks in volume. Here's how to massage your greens:

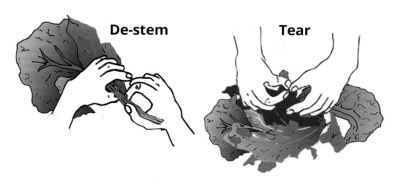

De-stem

Tear

Add:

1 tbsp lemon juice (fresh squeezed)

1 tbsp olive oil

¼ tsp sea salt (or other)

Massage

Massage kale with all ingredients for 2 to 5 minutes until kale looks vibrant, softened and supple. Finish with remaining dressing. Add toppings of choice.

Peas

Storage: Store unwashed peas in the refrigerator in a container that allows air circulation. They will last a few days.

Ways to Enjoy Peas

- baked
- casserole
- dip
- mashed
- raw
- salad
- sauteed
- soup
- steamed
- stir fried

Kitchen Tools

- blender
- food processor
- hands (to shell)
- masher
- steamer
- wok

Good Partners

- basil
- cayenne
- cumin seed
- curry
- dill
- marjoram
- mint
- mustard seed
- nutmeg
- onion
- parsley
- rosemary
- sage
- tarragon
- turmeric

Did You Know ?

The Latin name for peas is pisum sativum. Peas are another superfood and are now grown all over the world. The oldest pea was 3000 years old and found in Thailand. The Romans grew 37 varieties of peas. In England they enjoy a dish called mushy peas. China considers the young tendrils and leaves of the pea plant a delicacy. Today, Canada is one of the largest producers and exporters of peas.

Do you know what shelling peas or "pea in the shoe" means?

Kerala Spiced Peas

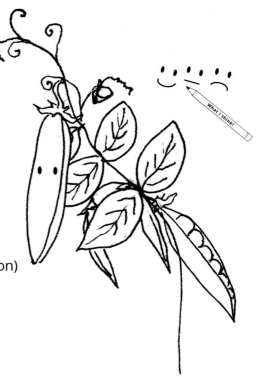

What You Need:

1 lb frozen petite peas
1 medium onion, sliced
2 Tbsp fresh ginger, minced
3 cloves garlic, minced
2 tsp ground cumin
½ tsp ground coriander
½ tsp ground cardamom (or a dash of nutmeg & cinnamon)
½ tsp dry mustard
1 lemon, juiced, or about 3-4 Tbsp
2-3 Tbsp butter or ghee
Cilantro or grated lemon peel for garnish
Salt and pepper to taste

What You Do:

1. Melt butter or ghee in a heavy pan over medium to high heat.
2. Add onions and saute them until softened.
3. Add garlic, ginger, and all spices, and saute for 3-5 minutes.
4. Add peas, and cook until ingredients are hot and spices meld.
5. Stir in lemon juice.
6. Add salt and pepper to taste. (If desired, garnish with cilantro or grated lemon peel.)

Serves 4.

Green peas are green because they are picked when immature; their ripe color is more yellow. There are two kinds of peas: field peas and sweet peas. Field pea seeds are smooth and best for dried use. Sweet pea variety seed is wrinkled and best consumed when young.

Peas are considered to be pulses, which are crops that help improve the soil by fixing nitrogen. This makes them an environmentally-friendly crop.

The proper etiquette for eating peas is squashing them with the back of your fork.

What I think!

Peas Please Pasta!

What You Need:

1 16-ounce package small shell or elbow pasta
2 garlic cloves, chopped and crisped
2 Tbsp olive oil
¾ cup half and half
¾ cup whole milk
1 16-ounce package frozen petite peas (Do not thaw.)
2¼ cups freshly grated Parmesan cheese plus additional for serving
¼ cup sesame seeds
½ cup Italian parsley, chopped and divided
Salt and pepper to taste   (We add a bit of crushed red pepper.)

What You Do:

1. Crisp the garlic in 2 Tbsp of olive oil; remove and drain on a paper towel.
2. Cook pasta in a large pot of boiling salted water until it's just al dente, stirring occasionally.
3. Drain, reserving ½ cup of pasta cooking liquid. Return pasta to the pot.
4. Bring the cream and milk to simmer in a large skillet over low-medium heat. Add peas and cook until heated through, 1 to 2 minutes. It's important not to overheat the cream because it will separate.
5. Add 2¼ cups of cheese and stir until it's melted and sauce thickens slightly, about 1 minute.
6. Stir in ¼ cup of parsley.

7. Pour sauce over pasta along with sesame seeds and crisped garlic, and toss to coat. You may add some of the pasta cooking liquid, by the tablespoon, if dish is dry.
8. Season to taste with salt and pepper, and transfer to a serving bowl.
9. Sprinkle pasta with remaining 1/4 cup parsley.
10. Serve with additional Parmesan cheese.

Serves 4-6.

Variation: Add ⅛ tsp nutmeg. Try grated carrots or chopped raw red peppers.

Al dente is an Italian word that literally means "to the tooth." This term is used to describe the perfectly cooked pasta that still has a bit of chewiness to it. In college we would throw a strand of spaghetti on the wall, and if it stuck it was finished. If it fell off the wall it needed to cook a bit longer. The starches released from cooking pasta make something like glue, allowing the noodles to adhere to the wall. Probably not chef-worthy advice, but we love doing this!

What I think!

Spring Pea Dip

What You Need:

2 cups frozen peas

2 Tbsp ginger, grated or to taste

½ cup almonds or walnuts

1½ to 2 cups cilantro (leaves and stems)

1 Tbsp lemon or lime juice

2 Tbsp olive oil

Pinch of salt

What You Do:

Put everything in the blender or food processor and blend until smooth or to desired consistency.

Serves 4-8.

Variations: Try 2 Tbsp tahini, 1/4 cup mint or basil leaves, 1 clove garlic, ½ cup ricotta cheese, 1/3 cup Parmesan cheese, and/or 3 Tbsp sour cream.

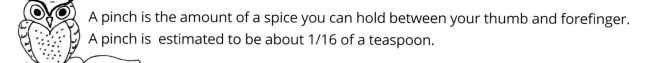

A pinch is the amount of a spice you can hold between your thumb and forefinger. A pinch is estimated to be about 1/16 of a teaspoon.

What I think!

 spring pea dip

1.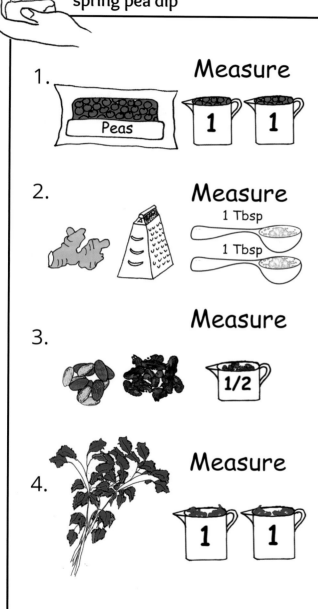

Measure

1 [cup] 1 [cup] **Peas**

2. **Measure**

1 Tbsp

1 Tbsp

3. **Measure**

1/2

4. **Measure**

1 1

5. **Squeeze** **Measure**

1 Tbsp

6. **Measure**

1 Tbsp

1 Tbsp

Olive Oil

7. **Pinch**

8. **Blend**

93

Stir Fried Peas

What You Need:

1-2 cups frozen or fresh peas (not canned)
1 cup corn, fresh, frozen, or canned
½ large red pepper, chopped
Kosher salt to taste
⬚ cup cooked quinoa or rice
2 Tbsp ginger, grated
2 Tbsp sesame oil
1 Tbsp stir fry sauce
⅛ tsp turmeric
Dash of anise seed to taste
Dash of cumin

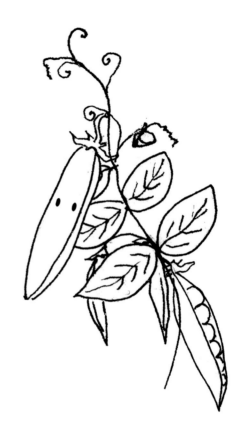

What You Do:

1. Chop large red pepper.
2. Grate ginger (the chunkier the better).
3. Stir fry red pepper in sesame oil.
4. Add corn and then peas.
5. Toss in stir fry sauce.
6. Add spices, including ginger, turning up heat a little so they get a bit crispy.
7. Remove from stove top and add cooked quinoa or rice.

8. Salt and pepper to taste. (We're big fans of Chinese red pepper.)

9. Serve hot or cold.

Serves 4.

Variation: Use 2 tsp soy sauce and 1 tsp vinegar and a good pinch of sugar in place of stir fry sauce.

There are generally 3 types of sweet peas that we eat. They are part of the legume family, which means they form pods with edible seeds inside. There are the fresh garden pea (spring - early winter), snap peas (late spring-early summer), and snow peas. Only the snow pea can be found throughout the year

What I think!

Sweet Potato

Storage: Store this vegetable in a dry, cool and well-ventilated location, but not in the refrigerator. They should last 3 to 5 weeks.

Ways to Enjoy Sweet Potatoes

- baked
- boiled
- casserole
- grilled
- juiced
- mashed
- pie oven fries
- steamed
- quesadilla

Kitchen Tools

- blender
- food processor
- fork
- fry cutter
- juicer
- knife

Good Partners

- allspice
- cardamom
- cinnamon
- chili pepper
- citrus
- cloves
- coconut milk
- dill
- garlic
- ginger
- ketchup
- maple syrup
- mustard
- nutmeg
- parsley
- paprika
- rosemary
- sage
- sesame oil
- smoked salt
- soy sauce
- sumac
- thyme
- white miso

Did You Know ?

Sweet potatoes come in white, **brown,** yellow, orange, **red,** and **purple** varieties.
They contain Vitamins A and C, which work well together to promote skin's good health.
When your complexion is dull, sweet potatoes can help you look better. When you eat the skin, this vegetable is also high in fiber. The whole plant is edible.
Did you know sweet potatoes are also a great dog treat when given in moderation?

Coconut Curried Sweet Potato and Kale

Adapted from America's Test Kitchen's *The Complete Vegetarian Cookbook.*

What You Need:

3 Tbsp olive oil, divided

1 onion, chopped

2 lbs sweet potato, peeled and sliced into ½-inch cubes

5 garlic cloves, minced

2-3 tsp ginger, grated or minced

1 to 1½ tsp sweet curry powder

2 large bunches of kale, destemmed and chopped

1 cup vegetable or chicken broth (We used Better than Bouillon.)

1 14-ounce can full-fat coconut milk, divided

1 Tbsp lemon or lime juice

⅓ cup pepitas (green pumpkin seeds), toasted

Salt to taste

Black pepper, freshly ground to taste

Red pepper flakes (optional), to taste

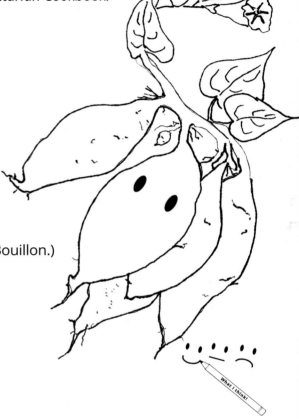

What You Do:

1. Toast pepitas in a medium skillet over medium-low heat, stirring frequently, or place on a cookie sheet and toast in the oven at 375°F until they're just golden. Set aside.
2. Warm 1 Tbsp of olive oil in a heavy pot over medium heat until shimmering. Add onion and cook for 5 minutes, stirring frequently.

3. Add sweet potatoes and cover, stirring to prevent sticking, for about 5 minutes. Put aside in a bowl.
4. Add remaining 1 Tbsp of olive oil to pot and heat to medium.
5. Add garlic, ginger, and curry powder, stirring constantly for 30 seconds.
6. Add half of kale and stir until wilted, about 1 minute.
7. Add remaining kale, broth, all but ½ cup of coconut milk, and ½ tsp of salt (or to taste). Cover pot, reduce heat to medium-low and cook, about 12 minutes, stirring occasionally.
8. Pour sweet potato mixture into pot, cover and continue to cook 10-20 minutes until tender.
9. When kale-sweet potato mixture is tender, remove lid and increase heat to medium-high until much of the extra liquid is cooked off, about 5 minutes.
10. Remove from heat and stir in remaining coconut milk. Add lemon/lime juice and season with salt, pepper and red peppers to taste.
11. Serve over rice and sprinkle with pepitas, sunflower seeds, sesame seeds, or pine nuts.

Serve with jasmine or basmati rice. This recipe tastes great the day after it's made.

Serves 6-8.

Stews are generally thicker than soups and may even be eaten with a fork from a plate. They can be made with vegetables, meat, poultry, mutton or seafood. The making of delicious and flavorful stews requires patience, as a long cooking time is necessary. Geographical location also plays a large role in how a stew is made: the colder the climate, the heartier the stew. In warmer climates, stews will generally be spicier, helping to cause perspiration which will cool the body. Burgoo is a stew associated with the harvest season. The true test of a burgoo is whether one's spoon can stand up in it.

What I think!

Sweet Potato Happy Cakes

Adapted from *Serious Eats*

What You Need:

1 cup mashed sweet potato (cooled)
1 egg
½ cup sour cream or plain yogurt
1¾ cup milk
1 Tbsp honey
1 tsp vanilla
2 Tbsp melted butter
1 cup white flour
¾ tsp baking powder
¼ tsp baking soda
¼ tsp salt
¼ tsp of cinnamon
Pinch of nutmeg
Oil for frying pancakes

What You Do:

1. In a medium bowl, mix wet ingredients.
2. In a larger bowl, mix all dry ingredients.
3. Slowly add wet mixture to dry ingredients, gently fold in. Do not overmix.

4. Heat oil in a skillet. When hot, ladle batter into small batches to make 3- to 4-inch pancakes. Cook several minutes on each side until pancakes are cooked through and golden brown. (watch for bubbling and edges getting crisp)

Serve warm with a dusting of powdered sugar or syrup.

Variations: You may use 2¼ cups of buttermilk in place of milk and sour cream. ½ tsp. pumpkin pie spice can replace the above spices. Try using whole wheat flour; pancakes will be more dense.

Makes 12 small pancakes.

To drizzle means to rain lightly or pour evenly and slowly, often referring to oil or honey being patiently incorporated into a mixture. A drizzle can also be a garnish for a soup or dish, such as a drizzle of balsamic vinegar.

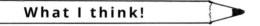

What I think!

Sweet Tattie Oven Fries

What You Need:

1 large sweet potato, scrubbed

Olive oil in a sprayer

Ice water

1 tsp cornstarch

Paprika to taste

Salt to taste

Pepper to taste

Oregano or spice of your choice

1 brown paper bag

What You Do:

1. Preheat oven to 450°F.
2. Slice lengthwise. (You may want to cut fries in half if they are too long and too hard for small hands to handle.)
3. Soak fries in ice water for 10 minutes to help crisp them. Dry on paper towels.
4. Add 1 tsp of cornstarch into paper bag and toss potatoes around until coated.
5. Season with salt, pepper, paprika and a dash of oregano.
6 Spray fries with olive oil on a cookie sheet lined with parchment.
7. Separate fries on the cookie sheet. Don't allow potatoes to touch each other; they're fussy that way!
8. Bake for 20 to 30 minutes, or until fork tender.

9. Open oven, but leave potatoes in oven to crisp and allow steam to escape for 10 minutes.

Serves 3 kids or 2 adults.

Variation: You can toss sweet potato pieces in a bag with oil and seasoning. You do not need to peel the sweet potato. While still warm, try topping fries with grated mozzarella or parmesan cheese. Goes great with our **Tomato Blackberry Ketchup.**

Sweet Potato Treats for Dogs (from my dog Dalai to yours)

Slice sweet potatoes thinly and uniformly (1 in thick) and place on cookie sheet. Bake in low oven at 250° for about three hours until dry. Flip rounds and rotate baking sheet as needed. When fully cooled store treats in a jar with pet's name.

Scarlet Tuber Salad

What You Need:

4 medium potatoes, red or Yukon gold (about 3 cups)*
1 large sweet potato (about 2 cups), peeled
¼ to 1 cup mayonnaise
1 tsp yellow dijon or spicy whole grain mustard
1½ Tbsp apple cider vinegar
1 Tbsp honey
1 tsp of dill, fresh or dried
2 pickles, dill or sweet, chopped
2-4 Tbsp pickle juice
¼ tsp smoked paprika (or sweet)
Salt and pepper to taste

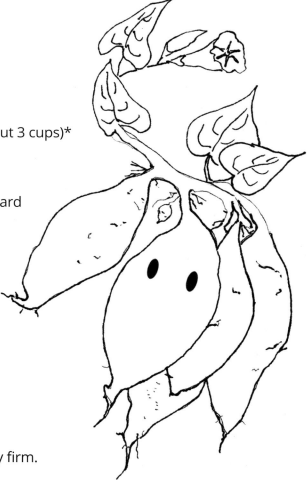

What You Do:

1. Boil potatoes whole until they're slightly firm.
2. Cool and slice potatoes.
3. Whisk all dressing ingredients together and pour over potatoes.
4. Toss gently with a spatula to coat, and adjust seasonings if needed.
5. Refrigerate and let flavors meld.
6. Before serving, sprinkle more dill, paprika or parsley over the top to give it a colorful and appetizing look.

Variations: Add onion, chopped celery, hard boiled eggs, bell pepper or bacon. Try with our **Zucchini Pickles** recipe. Peas, grated carrot, and scallions are also good. Tastes better second day.

*Waxy, not dry potatoes work best.

Serves 6.

What I think!

Tomato

Storage: Tomatoes have a longer shelf life if stored stem side down. Green tomatoes will ripen if you store them in a paper bag or a container that closes. Add an apple or a banana, and keep it out of sunlight for faster results. **Do you know why?**

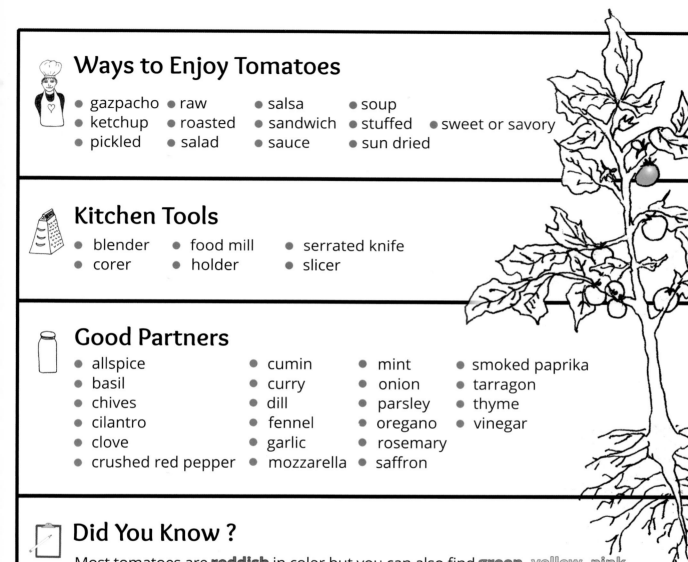

Ways to Enjoy Tomatoes

- gazpacho
- ketchup
- pickled
- raw
- roasted
- salad
- salsa
- sandwich
- sauce
- soup
- stuffed
- sun dried
- sweet or savory

Kitchen Tools

- blender
- corer
- food mill
- holder
- serrated knife
- slicer

Good Partners

- allspice
- basil
- chives
- cilantro
- clove
- crushed red pepper
- cumin
- curry
- dill
- fennel
- garlic
- mozzarella
- mint
- onion
- parsley
- oregano
- rosemary
- saffron
- smoked paprika
- tarragon
- thyme
- vinegar

Did You Know ?

Most tomatoes are **reddish** in color but you can also find **green**, yellow, **pink**, **brown**, black and white ones. In the Spanish town of Buñol, people gather to partake in the biggest annual tomato fight in the world. Twenty thousand people gather to throw 150,000 squishy tomatoes at each other. Sounds messy!

Did you know Heinz ketchup has a "speed limit"? During factory tests, ketchup cannot pour out of the bottle faster than .028 miles per hour or it is rejected.

Saucy, Sassy Marinara

What You Need:

¼ cup olive oil

4 cloves garlic, chopped

A handful of both chopped basil and oregano (Fresh is always best.)

Ground anise (optional)

Crushed red pepper (optional)

1 28-oz can of imported Italian tomatoes (Any crushed tomatoes will do.)

Salt and pepper to taste

¼ cup red wine or, if you prefer, ¼ cup vegetable broth

Grated fresh Parmesan cheese to taste

What You Do:

1. Place olive oil in large saucepan over medium heat and toss in garlic. Saute until garlic is crisp and brown.
2. Add tomatoes to oil and garlic, including juice.
3. Add oregano. (We like a little anise spice in our marinara. Give it a try; it tastes a bit like you have sausage in the sauce!)
4. Add ¼ cup red wine (or you can use veggie broth or water) to tomatoes. (Don't worry, Mom. The alcohol cooks away.)
5. Bring mixture to a boil, and then lower heat to a simmer and cook sauce until it thickens, about 45 to 60 minutes. Watch for sticking and stir as needed.

6. Add chopped basil and grated Parmesan cheese at the very end, stirring in and cooking for 1 minute more. Sprinkle cheese over top when serving.

Serve with pasta, Ricotta Balls, "Collie Flower" Pizza, zucchini, polenta or anything you enjoy with tomato sauce. We use this sauce when making meatball sandwiches on rolls. Yum!

Serves 4.

Variations: We like spice, so we add a bit of crushed red pepper. Try basil pesto instead of fresh basil.

What I think!

Snowball Tomato Soup

What You Need:

2 Tbsp butter

1 medium onion, thinly sliced

½ tsp salt

28-oz can crushed tomatoes or 5 cups diced fresh tomatoes

1 ½ cup chicken stock or vegetable broth

1-2 cloves garlic

2 sprigs fresh basil (about 8 leaves or so) chopped, or pesto to taste

One cup cooked rice (it's the snowball)

What You Do:

1. Warm butter in a wide-bottomed pan over medium heat.
2. Add onion and sprinkle with salt. Stir to coat and let cook until just starting to soften, about 5 minutes, stirring regularly.
3. Add tomatoes and garlic; stir and cover.
4. Turn heat to low and simmer for about 10-15 minutes or until tomatoes are broken down. Cool slightly.
5. Puree in a blender or food processor with basil until very smooth.
6. Serve warm.
7. As an added treat, spoon cooked rice into a small ladle (pack tightly) and turn upside down into soup bowl. Then ladle soup around rice, and there you have a "snowball."

Serves 2-4.

Variations: Add 1 small to medium diced, roasted sweet potato or cooked carrot before blending. A small handful of shredded mozzarella melts nicely and makes goop on top of soup. For cream of tomato soup, substitute broth with milk (do not let boil), or add a dollop of sour cream/yogurt at the finish. If basil isn't available, use a Tbsp of pesto.

Soup is of Germanic origin and is primarily a liquid food served hot or cold. Soups are generally classified into two main groups: thick or clear. Soups are an ancient food, dating back to 20,000 BC. Before pots could hold and boil water, soups were made by adding hot stones to liquids. Broths, bouillon, consomme, gazpacho, borscht, bisque and chowder are all soups. Science helped make soups more portable. Dehydrated soups that just needed water added were called pocket soups. These soups were helpful in keeping cowboys, soldiers and astronauts fed on the trail, the battlefield, or in outer space.

What I think!

Tomato Strawberry Salsa

What You Need:

6 medium fresh tomatoes, chopped (sort of chunky)
¼ cup mild onion, finely minced or sauteed
 (We prefer Walla Walla, but any mild onion will do.)
2 Tbsp mild green chilies (Make it easy--use canned.)
½ cup of red or yellow pepper, chopped
1 Tbsp honey
½ cup strawberries, chopped (A nice blend for young palates--sweet and savory.)
1 to 2 cloves garlic, chopped finely
1 tsp ground cumin
1 tsp salt
Dash of red or black pepper, to taste
1 Tbsp lime juice or balsamic vinegar
Handful cilantro, chopped

 What You Do:

Process all ingredients in a food processor to your desired consistency. No food processor?
A blender or hand chopping and mixing is our preference.

Variations: Try sauteing the onions to sweeten the salsa. You can experiment with other fruits
such as peaches, pineapple, mangos, or nectarines.

Salsa comes from the Spanish word for sauce, but it originated with the Incan people. It was made by combining tomatoes with chili peppers and ground squash seeds. The wild tomato comes from Ecuador and Peru; however, it was the Central Americans and Aztecs who domesticated the tomato. Salsa has been America's favorite condiment since 2000.

What I think!

Tomato Tarte Tartin

Adapted from Melissa Clark's recipe from the *New York Times Online*

What You Need:

2 pints grape and/or cherry tomatoes. An assortment of colors
is nice.
1 large red onion, sliced thinly
Pinch of sugar
1 sheet thawed puff pastry, cut into a 9- to 10-inch circle (We used
Pepperidge Farm.)
2 Tbsp butter
2 Tbsp chopped fresh basil (May substitute 2 tsp dried basil.)
1 Tbsp chopped fresh thyme (May substitute 1 tsp dried thyme.)
Vegetable oil spray or oil mister
½ tsp rice vinegar
2 Tbsp water
1 tsp cornstarch
Salt and pepper to taste

What You Do:

1. Preheat oven to 425°.
2. Melt butter in a 9- to 10-inch heavy ovenproof skillet. We use cast iron.
3. Place sliced onion in a skillet with a pinch of sugar. Saute onion until it's caramelized and lightly brown, stirring frequently, 10-15 minutes.

4. While onions cook, wash and drain tomatoes. Place tomatoes on a sheet pan when oven reaches temperature. Dry them in oven for 10-12 minutes.

5. When onions are done, remove from pan and set aside.

6. Mix water and rice vinegar, and stir in cornstarch with a fork.

7. In a bowl, stir water and vinegar mixture into tomatoes.

8. Add salt and pepper to taste.

9. Clean and dry same skillet, and apply oil spray.

10. Place ingredients in skillet in this order: tomato mixture, basil and thyme, onions, more salt and pepper, puff pastry.

11. Tuck puff pastry edges into the skillet.

12. Cut several long slits in the puff pastry.

13. Bake for 25 to 30 minutes, or until golden brown.

14. Allow tarte tartin to rest for about 10 minutes.

15. Run a knife along edge of skillet. Turn onto a platter or large cutting board.

16. Serve immediately.

Serves 6-8.

Tartin is a French dish made from fruit that is cooked until caramelized, added to a pastry and baked. It is named after the Tartin sisters, who created the apple tartin by mistake in their hotel 100 miles south of Paris in the 1880s. Good mistakes can happen too!

What I think!

Winter Squash

Storage: Choose a squash which is heavy, hard with a dull rind, not shiny. Squashes generally can be stored a long time. Smaller squashes can last a month or two, while larger squashes last 3-6 months. Keep dry and do not store in the refrigerator. A cool well-ventilated room around 50-55°F is best. Do not store with ripening fruits. Longer storage turns squash yellow and makes the inside stringy. Stems also help squash last longer.

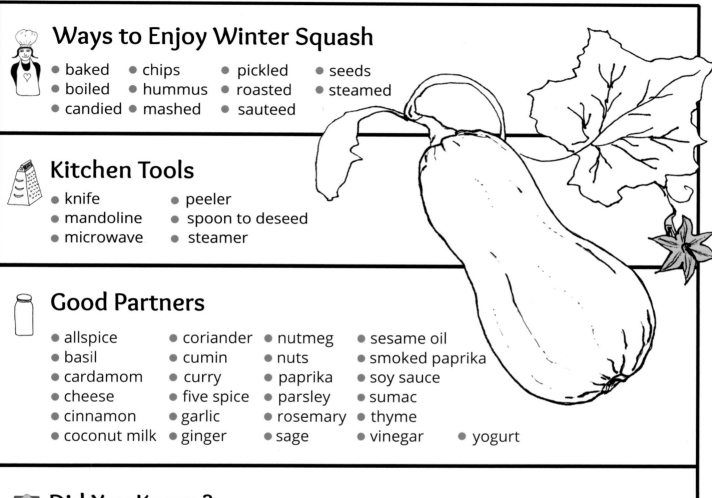

Ways to Enjoy Winter Squash

- baked
- boiled
- candied
- chips
- hummus
- mashed
- pickled
- roasted
- sauteed
- seeds
- steamed

Kitchen Tools

- knife
- mandoline
- microwave
- peeler
- spoon to deseed
- steamer

Good Partners

- allspice
- basil
- cardamom
- cheese
- cinnamon
- coconut milk
- coriander
- cumin
- curry
- five spice
- garlic
- ginger
- nutmeg
- nuts
- paprika
- parsley
- rosemary
- sage
- sesame oil
- smoked paprika
- soy sauce
- sumac
- thyme
- vinegar
- yogurt

Did You Know ?

The word squash comes from the Narragansett Indian word askutasquash, which means a "green thing eaten raw." Winter squashes are an excellent, healthy food that helps regulate blood sugars. The leaves, tendrils, shoots, stems, flowers, seeds and fruit are all edible. Squashes come in many colors, such as orange, yellow, white, green, tan, blue, and striped, and also come in a wide variety of sizes and shapes. *Did you know all squash skins and seeds are edible?*

117

Bigfoot Sas"squash" Mac 'n Cheese

What You Need:

1 cup cooked acorn (or other winter squash)
2 cups cooked macaroni noodles or noodles of choice
Dash of smoked paprika or nutmeg (optional)
1 tsp dry mustard powder (optional)
1 Tbsp butter
1 Tbsp flour
1 cup milk
½ cup cheddar cheese, grated

For the Cheese Sauce:

1 Tbsp butter
1 Tbsp flour
1 cup milk
½ cup shredded cheddar cheese

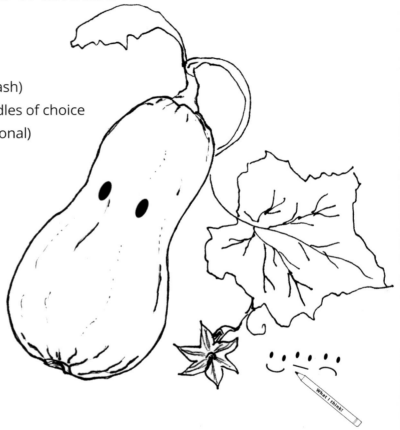

What You Do:

1. Cook your choice of pasta; rinse, drain and set aside.
2. Scoop out flesh of cooked squash. Mash or puree and set aside.
3. For cheese sauce, melt butter in a large heavy-bottomed saucepan and stir in flour.
4. Cook over low heat for about 30 seconds, stirring constantly.

5. Gradually stir in milk and spices (if desired).

6. Increase heat a little to bring the mixture to a gentle simmer.

7. Cook for 5 minutes, stirring constantly until mixture thickens.

8. Add squash to sauce and whisk until it's perfectly smooth.

9. Add grated cheese and stir until melted.

10. Add pasta and stir until combined.

Serves 4 Bigfoots or 6 Littlefoots.

Variations: Try with colby jack or gruyere cheeses instead of cheddar.

For safer cutting and peeling, you can microwave these hard squashes for 3-12 minutes. Be sure to cool before handling. Peel off the skin using a vegetable peeler or scoop out flesh with a large spoon.

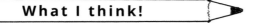
What I think!

Sunshine Hummus

What You Need:

½ cup cooked or canned squash
1½ Tbsp olive oil
1½ cups garbanzo beans
2 Tbsp tahini
1 clove garlic, pressed
1 lemon, juiced
¼ tsp smoked paprika
Dash of cumin
Salt and pepper to taste

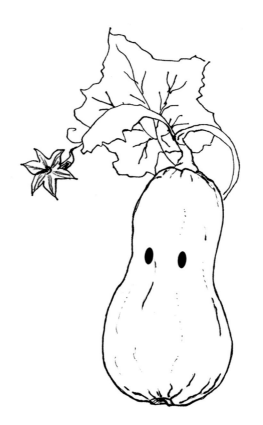

What You Do:

1. Place squash, oil, garbanzo beans, tahini, garlic and lemon juice in a food processor or blender and process until creamy.
2. Add seasoning and make any adjustments.
3. Store in refrigerator for about a week. Serve as a spread on sandwiches, or serve as a dip with crackers, vegetables, or our Sweet Potato Oven Fries.

Variations: For a more kid-friendly hummus, you may add a few ounces of cream cheese or some peanut butter. Hummus can be made from almost any vegetable, so feel free to substitute sweet potato or canned pumpkin for the squash. Hummus works well with many additions.

Serves enough for a party and leftovers can be refrigerated for about a week.

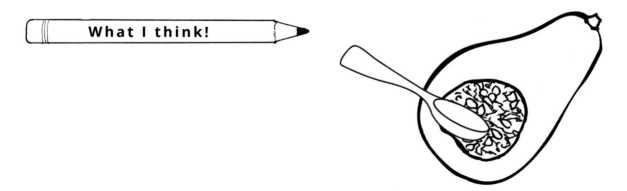

The origin of hummus is debatable, but the earliest mention of it in a cookbook dates back to the 13th century in Cairo, Egypt. The word hummus means chickpea in Arabic. Chickpeas are abundant in the Middle East and are a perfect food for the rugged arid climate found there. Chickpeas are also a nutritional powerhouse, high in protein, fiber, minerals and nutrients, filling almost all of a person's needs. Eaten with bread it forms a complete protein. In the modern world, hummus recipes incorporate numerous flavor variations.

What I think!

Dinner in a Hurry Curried Squash Soup

What You Need:

2½ lbs winter squash (We used Red Kuri, but you can use any type.)
1 medium sweet onion, chopped
1 tart apple, peeled, cored and chopped (We used Jonagold.)
1½-2 cups water, depending on dryness of the squash
½ cup coconut milk
1 Tbsp jarred vegetable or chicken stock (We used Better than Bouillon.)
1½ tsp sweet curry powder
2 Tbsp oil of choice
Salt to taste
Grated ginger to taste (optional)

What You Do:

1. Split winter squash and place in a small casserole dish or microwave-safe bowl face up. Microwave on high for 5-6 minutes.
2. Turn dish around halfway and microwave for 5-6 minutes more. When done, remove seeds and scoop squash out. Set aside to partly cool.
3. In a heavy pot, such as a Dutch oven, saute onions and apples in oil until golden brown.
4. Place onions and apples in a food processor or blender and pulse until smooth.
5. Add squash, water, and vegetable or chicken stock, and process until creamy. Add more water if necessary.

6. Pour mixture into heavy pot. Whisk in curry powder and coconut milk. If you use ginger, add it at this point. Simmer mixture for 15-20 minutes.

Serves 4-6.

Variations: You may serve soup with a dollop of plain yogurt, sour cream, chopped peanuts, cilantro, mint, etc. Let your imagination run wild!

What I think!

Dollop: A dollop is a glob or small blob of something, but often refers to a soft food used as a garnish or decoration placed on top of another food. Would you like a dollop of mud or a dollop of whipped cream on your pie?

Butternut Squash and Black Bean Quesadilla

What You Need:

4 - 8 tortillas (4 large or 8 small) - flour, corn or any personal preference
3 cups winter squash, diced - butternut, acorn, kabocha or delicata
2 tsp Moroccan harissa dry spice mix (or make our harissa recipe)
15 oz can black beans
6 Tbsp oil (more or less)
2 cups shredded Monterey cheese or cheddar
Salt to taste

What You Do:

1. Peel and dice squash. Heat 2 Tbsp of oil in a saute pan over medium-high heat. When oil is hot, add diced squash. (You may need to do this in two batches.)
2. Generously sprinkle Moroccan dry spice on squash and cook until it's brown and soft. Flip squash as it cooks to keep it from burning. The squash should caramelize but not be mushy. Set aside.
3. Drain and rinse 15 oz can of black beans, or use any variety you prefer, including refried.
4. Shred the cheese.
5. Heat a skillet and spray lightly with oil. (We use a nonstick pan.) Place a tortilla in pan and flip it after a few minutes.
6. Place generous amount of squash, beans and cheese on the heated large tortilla, and then cover with another tortilla.

7. Cook for several minutes until golden. Flip quesadilla and cook until other tortilla side is warm and golden in color.
8. Remove quesadilla from pan and slice it into desired sized wedges.
9. Serve with cilantro cream (see our recipe), salsa, guacamole and sour cream, if desired.

Serves 8 small appetizer plates, 6 lunch appetites or 3 dinner appetites.

Variations: Add any veggies you enjoy. Try sauteed kale, onions, bell peppers or corn. Add cilantro and chili peppers too. Fried rice is also nice.

A quesadilla is basically a portable pie. It is considered a Mexican food, but the tortilla has roots with the Native Americans. The addition of cheese comes from the Spaniards' influence in Mexico around the year 1520. The word queso translates to cheese in Spanish. In its simplest form, a quesadilla is a flatbread, called a tortilla, made from flour or corn, stuffed with cheese and heated in a hot dry skillet. When the cheese melts, the quesadilla is folded over like a turnover. In addition to cheese, a quesadilla can have a variety of filling options such as beans, potatoes, herbs, meat and vegetables. Generally the further south one goes in Mexico, the more complex the fillings become.

What I think!

Dry Harissa Seasoning

1 ½ tsp cumin, ground

1 ½ tsp coriander, ground

1 ½ tsp caraway, ground

1 ½ tsp fennel, ground or 1 generous tsp fennel seed (optional)

2 Tbsp chili powder (hot or not, your choice)

1 Tbsp smoked paprika (or reg if prefered)

1 tsp garlic powder

½ tsp salt

¼ tsp cinnamon, ground (optional)

Dash ginger, ground (optional)

Mix all ingredients together and store in a jar.

Harissa is a spice blend that can be either a chili paste or a dry herb mix. In Northern Africa and the Middle East it is used regularly. It is a great addition to dips, couscous, eggs, hummus, vegetables and grilled fish or meat. Add olive oil or butter to make a paste or sauce. Or try mixing with Greek yogurt as a vegetable, fish or meat topping. Vary seasoning amounts to personal taste.

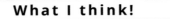

What I think!

Dry Harissa Seasoning

1. Cumin **Measure.**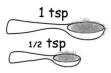
   1 tsp
   1/2 tsp

2.  Ground Coriander **Measure.**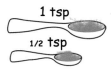
   1 tsp
   1/2 tsp

3. Ground Caraway **Measure.**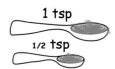
   1 tsp
   1/2 tsp

4. Ground Fennel **Measure.**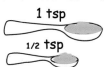
   1 tsp
   1/2 tsp

5.  Chili Powder **Measure.**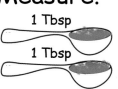
   1 Tbsp
   1 Tbsp

6. Paprika **Measure.**
   1 Tbsp

7. Garlic Powder **Measure.**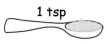
   1 tsp

8. **Measure.**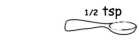
   1/2 tsp

9. Cinnamon **Measure.**
   1/4 tsp

10. **Measure.** Dash

11. **Mix.**

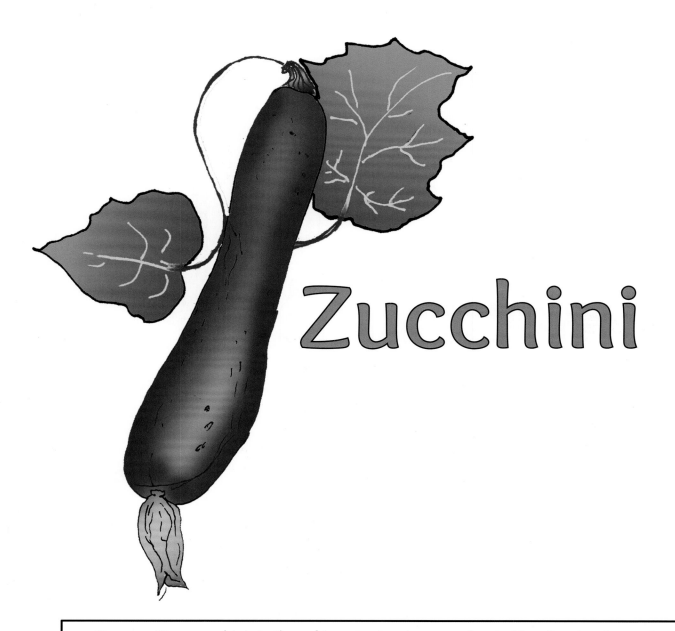

Zucchini

Storage: Store zucchinis in the refrigerator in a loose perforated bag for about a week

Ways to Enjoy Zucchini

- baked fries
- blossoms
- breaded
- chips
- grilled
- marinated
- pesto
- pickled
- raw
- roasted
- salad
- sandwich
- sauteed
- soup
- spiralized
- stew
- stuffed
- quiche

Kitchen Tools

- box grater
- knife
- manaka
- mandoline
- peeler
- spiralizer
- spoon or scoop

Good Partners

- basil
- chives
- coconut milk
- coriander
- cumin
- curry
- dill
- marjoram
- miso
- oregano
- crushed red pepper
- garlic
- sesame oil or seeds
- smoked paprika
- soy sauce
- tomatoes
- thyme
- turmeric
- Zaatar

Did You Know ?

The word zucchini comes from the Italian word zucca, which means squash. When picking a zucchini, look for the darkest green ones, which have the most nutrients. Zucchinis have more potassium than bananas, a mineral that helps regulate blood pressure, making it great for your heart. The most flavorful zucchinis are small to medium in size. Zucchini blossoms are also edible and delicious; often they are dipped in a batter and eaten tempura style.

Did you know that zucchini is also used in cosmetics and soap?

Zucchini Confetti Carrot Bread

What You Need:

2 eggs
⅓ cup melted coconut or vegetable oil (We used peanut oil.)
¼ cup Greek yogurt or unsweetened applesauce
½ cup light brown sugar
¼ cup white sugar
2 tsp vanilla
1-2 tsp cinnamon
½ tsp nutmeg
½ tsp powdered ginger
½ tsp allspice
1½ cups flour
½ tsp salt
¾ tsp baking powder
¾ tsp baking soda
1 cup zucchini, shredded, loosely packed
1 cup carrots, grated, loosely packed
½ cup walnuts or pecans, chopped (optional)
½ cup raisins (optional)

What You Do:

1. Preheat the oven to 350°F.

2. Grease and flour a 9x5 inch pan.

3. Whisk eggs with oil, yogurt/applesauce, sugars, and vanilla.

4. Mix all spices together and then whisk them into wet ingredients.

5. Sift together flour, salt, baking powder and baking soda. Fold flour mixture into wet ingredients, barely combining.

6. Gently fold both zucchini and carrots into batter.

7. Pour batter into pan and bake for about 55-60 minutes, or until a skewer or toothpick comes out cleanly. Begin to check around 45 minutes.

Serves 8-12.

Variations: You may substitute spices with 2-2½ tsp of pumpkin pie spice. Also, you can use 1/8 cup applesauce and 1/8 cup yogurt. You can try to replace brown sugar with ¼ cup honey for a denser, more moist cake. Sesame seeds sprinkled on top are tasty, nutritious, and adds texture.

What I think!

zucchini blossom

Korean Pancakes

What You Need:

2 cups yellow summer squash or zucchini, washed, deseeded, and grated
1½ cups carrots, peeled and grated
2 cups yellow potatoes, peeled and grated
¾ cup green onions, finely diced (about 4 onions)
¾ cup orange or red sweet pepper, finely diced (about 1 pepper)
2 cups all-purpose flour
1 large egg, beaten
¾ -1 cup chicken broth or water
1 tsp salt
¼ tsp black pepper
Vegetable oil or olive oil (for frying)
Sesame oil (for frying)

What You Do:

1. Grate squash, carrot and potatoes. (If you can use a food processor, it's much faster. If not, a box grater does just fine.) Place in a large mixing bowl.
2. Stir flour into vegetables until it is well distributed. Add egg and ¾ cup of liquid, and stir. If batter is very stiff, add remaining ¼ cup of liquid.
3. Stir in salt and pepper.

4. Heat ½ Tbsp of olive oil or vegetable oil in a skillet (we love an iron skillet, but any will do), and swirl to coat pan bottom. Place ¼ cup of batter in skillet and spread it until it's thin and evenly distributed (about ¼ inch).
5. Fry pancake until golden and crispy, raising pancake to allow oil to reach beneath. (This takes about 3-5 minutes.)
6. Flip pancake, and drizzle a small amount of sesame oil (⅛ tsp) around outside edge of pancake (to make it crispy).
7. Again, use a spatula to allow the oil to reach completely underneath pancake. Make sure that pancake is tender in center and very crispy on outside.
8. Remove pancake from skillet and place it on a plate covered with a paper towel to absorb any excess oil.

Continue process until all pancakes are cooked, adding extra vegetable oil or olive oil between batches as needed. (We like to keep the pancakes warm in the oven, but not too long or they will get soggy.) Serve with a splash of soy sauce or a favorite dipping sauce.

Serves 4-6.

What I think!

Zany Zucchini Oat Waffles

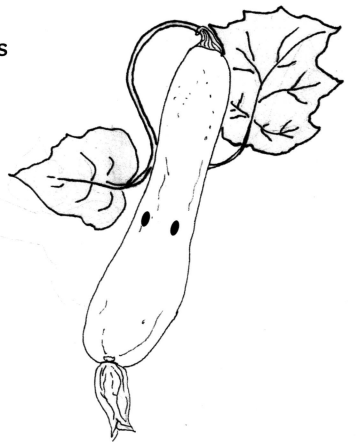

What You Need:

1 cup zucchini, finely shredded
1½ cups milk
2 eggs
2 Tbsp butter, melted
1½ cups flour, wheat, white or a flour mix
1 cup quick-cooking oats
1 Tbsp baking powder
2 Tbsp sugar
1 tsp salt
1½ tsp cinnamon
1 tsp vanilla

What You Do:

1. Place all wet ingredients into a large bowl and gently combine.
2. In another bowl, add all dry ingredients and mix well.
3. Slowly add dry ingredients into wet ones and gently stir. Do not overmix.
4. Heat a waffle iron and coat it with nonstick spray or oil. When it's hot, add a ladle of batter to the center of the iron. Cook until waffle is golden and crisp.

Serve with maple syrup or a dusting of powdered sugar. Leftover waffles freeze well and can be reheated in a toaster.

Serves 8.

Variations: They also go great with applesauce. Try adding ⅛ tsp nutmeg.

Though our eyes prefer big vegetables, in general, smaller vegetables are tastier. With extra large zucchini, it is often desirable to scoop out the soft, watery pulp. Very large zucchinis may also have bitter-tasting skins.

What I think!

Lip Smackin' Pickles

What You Need:

1 pint canning jar (or other glass jar)

1 or 2 small firm zucchini, thinly sliced

3 or 4 thin slices of onion

1 Tbsp fine salt (or pickling salt)

3 ice cubes

½ cup white or apple cider vinegar

1 cup sugar

1½ tsp mustard seeds

1 tsp mustard powder or prepared mustard

¾ tsp turmeric

½ tsp celery seed (optional)

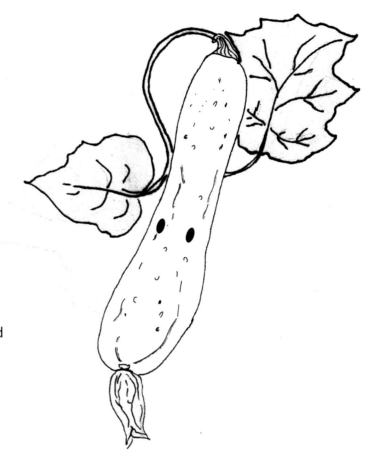

What You Do:

1. Slice zucchini and onion fairly thin, ⅛ inch thick, and place in a resealable bag.
2. Add enough water to cover vegetables.
3. Add salt and mix in bag until the salt dissolves.
4. Add a few ice cubes and wait about 1 hour.
5. Drain zucchini and onion slices and pat dry with paper towels or clean cloth.
6. In a pan, mix together vinegar and remaining ingredients. Bring to a simmer and stir to make sure sugar dissolves. Let pan cool.

7. Place vegetables in clean jar.

8. Add cooled brine, making sure brine completely covers vegetables.

9. Place jar in refrigerator for 24 hours before eating. Use pickles within one week.

Variations: Add a few carrot slices, cauliflower slices or red pepper. Add peppercorns, allspice berries or coriander seeds. Try adding some dill. A dash of red pepper flakes will add some heat. For crispy pickles without soaking, try Pickle Crisp granules. As an alternative add tomato, grape, raspberry, or horseradish leaves to the jar. Do you know why this works?

The largest zucchini measured 69.5 inches and weighed 65 lbs. Can you weigh and measure your zucchini? How many zucchinis tall are you?

What I think!

Spices and How to Use Them

There are many ways to improve, enhance or change the taste of vegetables. Roasting can mellow the flavor; massaging greens improves the texture; blanching can remove the raw taste; and younger vegetables naturally taste sweeter and milder. Spices, herbs and other flavorings also make dramatic differences in recipes. Vegetables all have unique taste qualities from sweet to bitter, earthy to grassy, and spicy. Sometimes vegetables fall into more than one category.

Spices have many characteristics, too--like smoky, sweet, pungent, woodsy, sour, hot, and bitter, to name just a few. Generally, if you like the spices in your recipe, then the pairings work.

As a general guide, you may refer to the following information for good pairings.

- Sweet vegetables partner well with spicy and warm flavors.(like sweet potatoes with cayenne and cinnamon).

- Strong-tasting vegetables partner well with strong herbs, spices and flavorings (like Brussels sprouts with thyme, cumin and balsamic vinegar).

- Mild or sweet vegetables partner well with bright and hot flavorings (like zucchini with basil, or red pepper flakes).

- Grassy or mild vegetables partner with almost anything (like green beans and nuts, mustard, lemon or rosemary).

- Earthy vegetables partner well with strong sharp notes (like beets with ginger and orange).

Adjustments to seasonings and substitutions can take a recipe to a whole new level. Decide for yourself how the vegetable tastes and use your nose to pick spice partners. Sometimes, before I jump in and flavor the whole batch, I set aside a bit of my recipe and experiment with it. Don't be afraid to experiment.

Be very careful when smelling scents--some can be overpowering. Sniff gently and from a distance.

Salad Dressings and Dipping Sauces

Very Berry Strawberry Vinaigrette Dressing

What You Need:

10 oz. fresh (or frozen) strawberries, 1 cup pureed
1 Tbsp honey (adjust amount of honey to sweetness of berries)
1 Tbsp balsamic vinegar or apple cider vinegar
1 Tbsp neutral tasting oil, (algae oil, avocado oil, extra virgin olive oil)
¼ tsp salt or to taste
¼ tsp ground black pepper (optional)

What You Do:

1. Rinse and destem berries. (Using a drinking straw works well to remove core.)
2. Mash and pulse in blender until there are no whole pieces (No worries; it doesn't hurt them).
3. Add remaining ingredients to food processor or blender and blend until smooth.
4. Clean and dry any pint size jar (dressing should last 3 to 5 days refrigerated).
5. When ready to serve, pour into jar and and do your "shaky dance."

Variations: Try with other fruits like raspberries or blueberries

The garden strawberry is a hybrid of the Chilean and the North American wild strawberry plant. The strawberry is not a true berry. The strawberry is the only fruit with seeds on the outside, with each strawberry having about 200 seeds.

What I think!

Very Berry Strawberry Vinaigrette Dressing

1. **Rinse.**

2. **De-stem.**

3. **Mash.**

4. **Pulse.**

5. **Add.** 1 Tbsp

6. **Add.** 1 Tbsp

7. **Add.** 1 Tbsp

8. **Add.** 1/4 tsp

9. **Add.** 1/4 tsp

10. **Shaky Dance.**

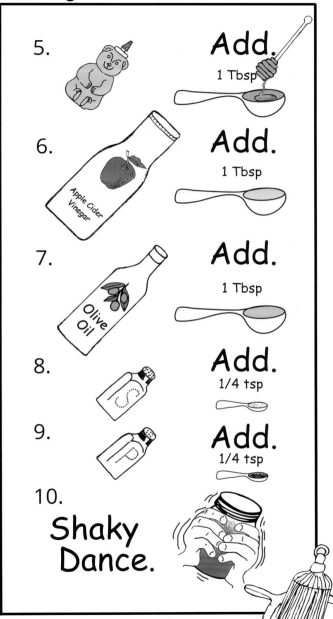

143

Apple Ginger Salad Dressing

What You Need:

1 clove garlic, pressed

2 Tbsp fresh lemon, juiced

2 Tbsp apple cider vinegar

2 Tbsp soy sauce

¼ cup extra virgin olive oil or avocado oil

½ cup apple juice

2 tsp grated ginger (or to taste)

What You Do:

Add everything into a jar, screw the lid on tightly, and do your "shaky dance".

Variations:

Add a splash of sesame oil, a little mustard, apple balsamic vinegar or a touch of honey!

What I think!

Apple Ginger Salad Dressing

1. Pressed.

2. Juice   Measure.

1 Tbsp
1 Tbsp

3. Measure.

1 Tbsp
1 Tbsp
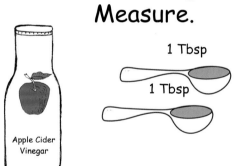

4. Measure.

1 Tbsp
1 Tbsp
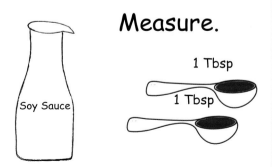

Soy Sauce

5. Measure.

 Olive Oil  1/4

6. Measure.

 Apple Juice  1/2

7. Grate   Measure.

 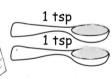 1 tsp
1 tsp

8. Shakey Dance

Lemon Drop Dressing

What You Need:

⅓ cup champagne vinegar
1 tsp fresh lemon, juiced *
5 tsp lemon, zested
3 cloves garlic, minced
2 tsp dijon mustard
¼ tsp salt

¼ tsp fresh ground black pepper
1 tsp oregano or dill   (We prefer dill
because it's milder)
½ cup extra virgin olive oil
½ cup full-fat yogurt or sour cream

What You Do:

1. Combine champagne vinegar, lemon juice, lemon zest, garlic, dijon mustard, salt, pepper, and oregano or dill in a bowl.
2. Slowly whisk olive oil into lemon juice mixture until thickened. Whisk yogurt or sour cream into mixture. Transfer dressing to a sealable container.
3. Refrigerate 15 minutes to overnight (this dressing tastes better after a rest). Dressing should last 3 to 5 days refrigerated

*We recommend that you use only freshly squeezed lemon juice. Fresh tastes best!
(It's a good blend for the champagne vinegar we love, but in a pinch substitute white or red vinegar.)

What I think!

146

Lemon Drop Dressing

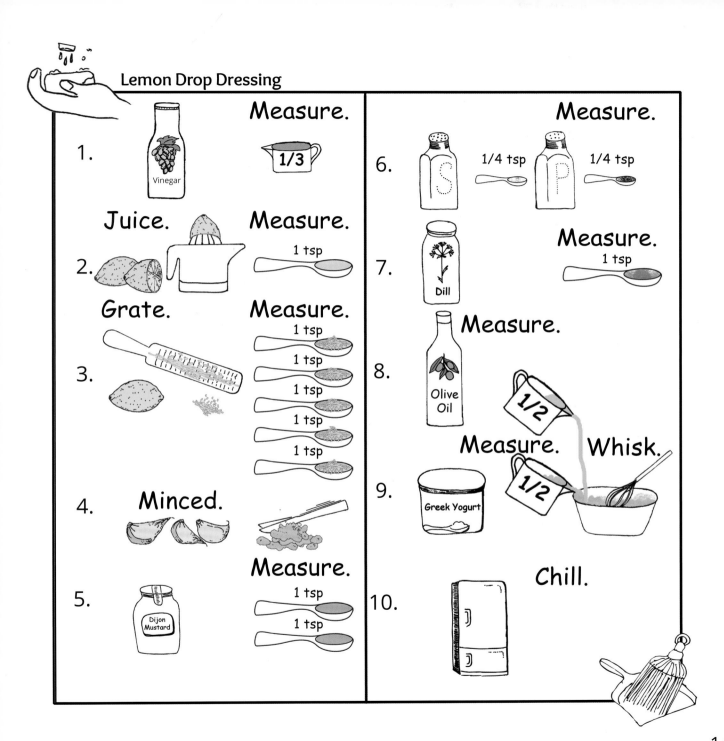

1. Vinegar — Measure. 1/3

2. Juice. Measure. 1 tsp

3. Grate. Measure. 1 tsp, 1 tsp, 1 tsp, 1 tsp, 1 tsp

4. Minced.

5. Dijon Mustard — Measure. 1 tsp, 1 tsp

6. S — 1/4 tsp, P — 1/4 tsp — Measure.

7. Dill — Measure. 1 tsp

8. Olive Oil — Measure. 1/2

9. Greek Yogurt — Measure. 1/2 — Whisk.

10. Chill.

147

Tzatziki Dressing

Adapted from *What Jew Wanna Eat*

What You Need:

1 cup plain Greek yogurt
1 large cucumber, seeded, chopped, and dried *
1 garlic clove
1 tsp extra virgin olive oil
1-2 Tbsp lemon juice
1 Tbsp dill or mint, chopped
Salt and pepper to taste

What You Do:

1. Peel and seed the cucumber and chop up. Dry between paper towels.
2. Chop garlic.
3. Put other ingredients with cucumbers and garlic in a food processor and pulse until gently blended.
4. Chill the mixture for at least one hour, and serve with pita bread, raw vegetables, or as a salad dressing (dressing should last 3 to 5 days refrigerated).

Serves 6-8.

* This recipe works best with an English cucumber because it is drier than standard ones.

Tzatziki Dressing

1. Measure.

2. Prepare: seeded chopped dried

3. Chopped.

4. Measure. 1 tsp

5. Measure. Juice. 1 Tbsp or 2 Tbsp

6. Measure. Chopped. 1 Tbsp

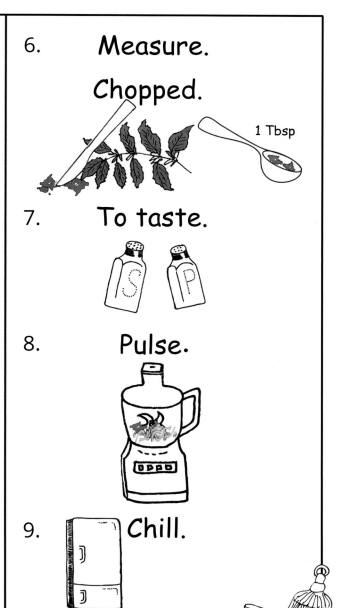

7. To taste.

8. Pulse.

9. Chill.

Cilantro Cream Sauce

What you need:

½ cup sour cream or Greek yogurt
Large handful cilantro leaves
1 Tbsp lime juice
2 cloves garlic
Salt to taste

What to do:

Place all the ingredients in blender and process until it's smooth. Drizzle the sauce over quesadillas for a pretty presentation. This dressing should last 3 to 5 days refrigerated.

What I think!

1. **Measure.**

2. **Measure.**
Large handful.

3. **Measure.**
Juice.

1 Tbsp

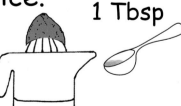

4.

5. **Measure.**
To taste.

Pulse.

6.

Chill.

Tomato Blackberry Ketchup

What You Need:

1 small can tomato paste

½ cup apple or white vinegar

¼ cup honey or maple syrup

¼ cup water

1 tsp salt

Handful of blackberries, pressed through a strainer or pressed

through cheesecloth to remove

seeds, or ½ tsp blackberry extract

½ tsp Worcestershire sauce

¼ tsp onion powder

¼ tsp ground black pepper

⅛ tsp garlic powder

⅛ tsp celery salt

⅛ tsp paprika

Pinch of ground cloves, optional

What You Do:

1. Mix all ingredients and cook on stovetop until simmering.
2. Turn down heat and gently cook for 25 minutes. Stir often.
3. Store in refrigerator when cooled.

Note: Commercial ketchups are often loaded with high-fructose corn syrup and preservatives. Making your own is a healthy, easy option. Homemade ketchup should last a good month in the refrigerator. To preserve longer, use the water bath canning method for about 15-20 minutes.

What I think!

What Children Learn from Cooking

Communication Skills and Working Together

We live in a communication age but, unfortunately, it is seldom taught to our children in school. Perhaps the most important life skill to develop and hone, good communication helps us to illuminate our ideas and bridge understanding with others.

Through the activity of shared cooking, we can ask questions along the way and discover a number of ways of accomplishing the same task. Working as part of a team lets us share meaningful work, become more flexible, and develop our own style ... all with delicious results. Cooking together also creates deep, fond memories. It's the perfect time to get to know your children and begin to build those essential life skills.

Math

Cooking and mathematics go hand in hand. For visual as well as kinetic learners, it's an opportunity to see how math works when using measuring utensils or a scale. Preparing food also requires a systematic approach to cooking (as in math); so organized thinking comes into play. Counting out the cutlery to set the table, measuring ingredients (fractions), setting a timer or converting recipe portions all are mathematical concepts vital to cooking. Ever wonder why there are a set of dishes to set the family table? Let's not forget to introduce food budgeting to your children as well; we can all eat affordably and well if we plan ahead and shop thoughtfully.

Hygiene and Safety

When you work in the kitchen you need to be safe and clean. Rolling up sleeves, washing hands, putting hair back and wearing an apron all help to set the stage and stress the importance of cleanliness and safety. Tailor tasks to be time and age appropriate. Always be clear about which tasks an adult will do, such as handling sharp knives or removing something from the oven. Gauge your child's individual readiness to work safely in the kitchen. To avoid frustration, start slowly and add more tasks incrementally.

Be sure to have everyone help with cleanup. Cleaning up is also part of cooking.

Nutrition - Better Health

Watch excess sugar, salt, and fat, and nurture your family and those you love with wholesome food for better health.

Nobody likes everything. Food becomes less scary and more approachable as children cook, handle, explore and learn about new foods. We do not recommend forcing children to eat; instead we use encouraging, nudging, and supporting approaches to encourage them to try new foods. A mouse's nibble or a brave bite will do it!

It tastes out of this world!

Science

Cooking is edible science. You experience texture and taste with your tongue. The chemistry and the physical changes we observe can be spellbinding. Have you watched batter rise into a glorious cake and think it's magic? Cooking blends science with art, making the learning possibilities endless. In cooking we can formulate a hypothesis, observe changes, connect cause and effect, and even adjust our outcomes. The step-by-step nature of cooking helps foster curiosity, patience and reasoning skills. Though recipes are designed to assure satisfactory and repeatable results, they do not have to be strictly followed. Change a recipe and see where it leads. Harvard has developed a science course, "Science and Cooking: From Haute Cuisine to the Science of Soft Matter ". Food and cooking are used to explain basic principles in applied physics and engineering. See *www.seas.harvard.edu/cooking/cooking archive* for more information.

Take your time. Observe

Reading

If you can read words or pictures, you can cook. What better way to show children the power of words? For pre-readers, pictures are writing, and as parents you can use simple drawings to communicate tasks with your young child. Cooking Vocabulary is varied, rich and unique in describing food and the processes food undergoes. Words like pop, drizzle, snickerdoodles, and noodles are fun words made for kids. We also recommend reading the recipe over with your child before cooking to ensure you both understand the sequence of events. Try making a visual grocery list, and include your child in shopping and make simple recipes charts for pre- and early readers.

Develop and Strengthen Motor Skills

Improving children's motor skills is key to helping them become confident, independent and better equipped to explore the world. Without strong hand-eye coordination skills, children may face limitations. Remember--little muscles tire quickly, so be patient. Confident little ones will love shaking homemade salad dressing in a jar, rolling dough, scooping and measuring ingredients, or cracking an egg or using a simple kitchen tool like a garlic press or egg slicer. When finished, let children help to wipe up the counter, wash a few dishes, put utensils away, and sweep the floor. All of these are great exercises to build up your child's self esteem. "I can do this!"

Creativity and Authentic Work

Perhaps the creative part of cooking is like the icing on the cake. We eat with our eyes first, so taking a little time to address aesthetics is very helpful in getting children interested in trying new things. Preparing a favorite dish, trying chopsticks, making decorations and garnishes, or having a picnic in the living room are just a few examples of activities that make food and eating more attractive and fun. Cooking is important work, involving all the senses, and it's a perfect match for children because they see the results of their efforts right away. When children help in the kitchen they see what's involved and learn to appreciate the effort that preparing food requires. Tell them how important eating healthy is and ask for their help. As they create food in the kitchen, you will see the pride they feel. Their mastery of tasks build competency, confidence and independence. Cooking teaches a child: "I am a valuable part of the family, I am needed."

Heide's Bio

My childhood recollection of foods is simple and seasonal. Though my mother made wonderful Austrian dishes, it is the love, pleasure and lovely way with which she served everything that made it magical. Even eating a baked potato for lunch was special with her. My mother often let me help her in the kitchen, and I cherish those memories when we worked side by side talking and laughing. She passed her gifts on to me.

As a parent I know having my son help in the kitchen proved invaluable. As a toddler, my son always helped to set our table and occasionally helped with the preparation. When he was a preschooler and we made tuna fish melts together, I remember him tasting it and saying, "it needs some lemon." Never underestimate our little ones, they are unstoppable! My son is now 20 and has a Pinterest account with recipes he collects and uses. To this day, we always put a squeeze of lemon in our tuna fish.

Are West-House

Although surrounded by a family of good cooks, Are became a "foodie" late in life, hanging out with women who loved to cook and enjoy good food, much of which harvested from the farms of beautiful Whidbey Island.

Her older sister, June, tells the story of a ten year-old Arlene baking a cake (on her own) for her dad's birthday. She had all the ingredients except butter. So, rather than forgo the cake or run to the neighbors to borrow butter, she substituted bacon drippings. Her sweet dad ate the cake (never mentioned it was probably disgusting) with a smile on his face, but probably a lump in his stomach. It was only after her dad passed (he didn't want her to feel bad) that she was told that "bacon drippings" didn't cut it as a substitute.

Marianne's Bio

Marianne grew up in a huge family where her dad was the main cook. Along with Polish-Ukrainian foods, she ate lots of wonderful Italian dishes like chicken cacciatore, veal scallopini, and lasagna. She remembers how many meals included a salad and how the family modified its diet when her dad's health dictated change. This is where she learned her love for food and health which inspired her to study Nutritional Science at Cornell University.

Following her work as a nutrition educator, Marianne has been a grade school teacher, counselor, photographer, and web designer. Marianne created 4waystoyummy.com, the website promoting this cookbook.

Marianne and her husband, John, are foodies, and they've cultivated a 17-year-old gourmand who has become quite expensive to maintain. Their kitchen is well-stocked with exotic spices, and they keep a steady veggie supply through CSA farms. She admits that John is probably the better cook.

Marianne remembers feeling overwhelmed with working, taking care of a child, keeping a home, and cooking dinner after a long day. She hopes that **4 Ways to Yummy** helps reduce stress for parents while providing nutritious, vegetable-based recipes.

Acknowledgement - Heide

We three friends/author of this book have put our all into it, and now it's time to present our beloved **4 Ways to Yummy** to the world. This project has been long in the making. When we discovered that there wasn't a book of healthy, fun, delicious vegetable recipes designed specifically for young people, we set about doing our best to fill that void. We sincerely hope you and your family enjoy it. I am so grateful to Are and Marianne for starting this journey with me and staying with me through all of the puddles and turns until the very end!

I would first like to thank my husband, Jerry, who was fully supportive of my project, and who (like myself) thinks everything is possible if you try hard enough and want it badly enough. He spent countless hours on the project and laid out the entire book. You are my best friend, with whom I could not have produced this book and with whom I share a full and happy life.

I also thank my son Shane and all of my friends for the inspiration, support and help they gave unconditionally. You are the spice of my life, and the icing on my "beet" cake.

Something we create is never ours entirely, and so I feel most grateful to our three editors, who willingly went over all the recipes and pages. To Ellen Michaud, Gene Koffkin and Robert J. Carlson: thank you for all of your hard work; you truly understood what was needed. I also must thank Sandra Lounsbery, MS, CN for her contributions to the project.

To my mother, who introduced cooking into my life in the most delightful way! I miss you, Mutti.

And lastly to my mini Schnauzer, Dalai... who attended every meeting and work session, without complaints, for almost three years! She's a good girl.

160

Symbols and Tips

Ways to Enjoy

We list many ways to prepare vegetables; now it's up to you to discover how different they can taste in a recipe. Kale smoothie and kale salad, for example, taste very different! A person may not like one but love the other, proving no vegetable should be considered a closed door. Model adventurous eating with your child by taking a brave bite or a mouse's nibble. Enlisting a little "food courage" may be necessary! Studies show that as we grow up, our taste buds evolve with exposure to different foods. Do color our pages! (Only use colored crayons or pencils.)

Kitchen Tools

Using a variety of kitchen tools helps children develop fine motor skills and critical thinking. Kitchen tools like a box grater can change the texture in a recipe, making it more kid-friendly and palatable. Sometimes you won't even know there are vegetables in a recipe (like adding grated summer squash to stews or spaghetti, or adding greens to smoothies). Kitchen tools that are age-appropriate are a wonderful gift for your child. Children having their own tools creates a sense of ownership for a cooking project, and they will learn to care for them.

Good Partners

We've added a list of spices and flavorings that pair well with the vegetables in our cookbook awe have included a **Spices and How to Use Them** page. Having a reference page of options makes it easy to alter and adjust our recipes when preparing them for your family. We don't all like the same thing and we don't have too! Make cooking more interesting by learning new things and experimenting!

Symbols and Tips

Did You Know?

Our clipboard icon marks this category, which is a mishmash of facts--some historical, bizarre or practical. But don't stop here. Check out healthy cooking books from your library and learn more. Take a cooking class, ask a good cook for a lesson, or have a veggie potluck party. Cooking is easier than you think, and the kitchen is where everyone belongs!

Recipes and Reflections

Each recipe features an illustrated vegetable that represents the primary vegetable in the dish. Each drawn vegetable has eyes but no facial expression, allowing your child to rate the recipe after sampling. You'll find the pencil icon next to the first vegetable on each recipe as a reminder. What's most important is honesty and exploration of children's likes and dislikes. There may be a simple fix! So much learning happens in this process.

Rainbow

We've even made it possible for our pre-readers to lead or follow along with our 12 drawn recipes. These recipes have been marked with a rainbow icon in the Table of Contents.

Some of our recipes include our owl. The owl provides an interesting fact, tidbit, history or word origin about the dish. We think he's smart and cute. Please give our owl a name and email it to us at www.4waystoyummy.com !

Symbols and Tips

What I Think

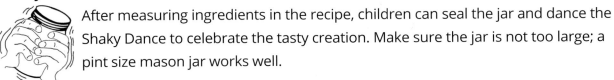 We have included a space for personal notes below the pencil icon on each recipe. By reflecting after preparing each recipe, you can adapt a recipe to make it taste the very best for your family. Rate how easy the recipe was to prepare. Who helped with food prep, ate it, and what did they think? Would you like to change anything next time? Let the children experiment, too. If they want carrots on their PB sandwiches, who can complain?

Hand Washing

Cleanliness is part of safety, and so we've included a hand-washing icon on each of our drawn recipes. Tying back hair and wearing an apron or a parent's t-shirt can help set the stage for the importance of cooking. Making this a habit is by far the best way to keep children healthy. We surely want that!

Salad Dressings and Sauces

We've included four tasty salad dressings and two sauces that also make great dips for fresh cut vegetables. They all have an accompanying drawn recipe so that young ones can read along when preparing. These recipes are perfect first recipes for children to learn. Soon they will able to make daily salads on their own.

Shaky Dance

After measuring ingredients in the recipe, children can seal the jar and dance the Shaky Dance to celebrate the tasty creation. Make sure the jar is not too large; a pint size mason jar works well.

Kitchen Memories